the greatest stories ever told

the greatest stories ever told

volume one:
great encounters with GOD

GREG LAURIE

great encounters with GOD

Library of Congress Cataloging-in-Publication Data
1 2 3 4 5 6 7 8 9 10 /11 10 09 08 07 06

ISBN: 0-9777103-5-1
Published by: Allen David Publishers—Dana Point, California
Coordination: FM Management, Ltd.
Cover design by Chris Laurie
Designed by Highgate Cross + Cathey
Printed in the United States of America

contents

chapter one

encounter in paradise: resisting the tempter

In the immortal words of Julie Andrews, *"Let's start at the very beginning, a very good place to start…."*

When it comes to *The Greatest Stories Ever Told*, no book ever written holds a candle to the Bible. And within the pages of Scripture, no stories are more foundational, more sweeping in scope, and more bursting with insights than those found within the book of Genesis. Six of the eleven dramatic encounters with God described in this book are drawn from the first book of the Bible.

Genesis is the book of beginnings. Just think of all the origin accounts woven through its fifty chapters…

Genesis records the origin of the universe. The first book of the Bible stands alone in accounting for the actual creation of the space-mass-time continuum which constitutes our physical universe.

Genesis declares the origin of the solar system. The Earth, as well as the sun, the moon, the planets, and all the stars of heaven, were likewise brought into existence by the Creator.

Genesis describes the origin of man. The widely believed theory of evolution is a complete illusion. The true record of man's beginnings is given only in Genesis, detailing man's creation, purpose, and uniqueness.

Genesis details the origin of marriage. God's unique and special plan for the man and woman is given. We also have the origin of the family—the basic infrastructure for any successful culture and society.

Genesis chronicles the origin of language—language in general, and also the various national languages in particular.

Genesis speaks to the origin of government. The development of organized systems of human government is described in

Genesis, with man being responsible not only for his own actions, but also for the maintenance of orderly social structures through systems of laws and punishments.

Finally, *in Genesis, we have the origin of evil.*

Many believe and teach that man is basically good, and when he does bad things, it's the result of his environment or outward circumstances. If you believe this, you must have a hard time making sense of this wicked world. The Bible teaches that man is basically sinful, and does bad things as a reflection of his true nature. We're not sinners because we sin, but rather we sin because we are sinners. It comes naturally.

And the third chapter of Genesis tells the story of how it all started. It is truly a great story. Although the account is unspeakably sad, it also reveals a God who is determined to seek and save His lost and finest creation: humankind.

adventures in paradise

I heard the story of a pastor who had just moved into a new town and wanted to get to know some of the people in his congregation. So one Saturday he went out to visit, paying pastoral calls on many people from his new church.

All was going well until he came to a house where he could clearly see someone was home—but they wouldn't answer the door. He knocked and knocked again, but no one came to answer it. So, with a little smile, he took out one of his business cards and wrote *Revelation 3:20* on the back, and stuck it in the door. You know the verse: "Behold, I stand at the door and knock. If anyone hears My voice and opens the door, I will come in to him and dine with him, and he with Me."

The next day at the morning church service, after the offering was counted, an usher found the pastor's card that he left on that person's door with another biblical reference below his.

It was Genesis 3:10.

"And he said, 'I heard thy voice in the garden, and I was afraid, because I was naked: so I hid myself."

Adam and Eve had been placed in a veritable paradise. Adam's job description was to tend and keep the garden, discovering and marveling in all God had done, and walking in fellowship with Him.

Talk about having it made in the shade! This first couple was told they could eat of any tree in the garden—excepting only the Tree of the Knowledge of Good and Evil.

And yet there was Eve, hanging out by that very tree.

fatal attraction

Why is it that we are always attracted to that which can harm us? You tell a child to not touch a certain thing or go to a certain place and that's exactly where they will be when given a chance. It's human nature!

In our warped minds we think that God is keeping something good from us. Scripture, however, tells us: "No good thing will He withhold from those who walk uprightly."[1]

God gave them a warning label and they ignored it.

Warning labels exist because someone at some point did something stupid with a given product, injured themselves, sued the company, and quite possibly won.

These labels have become wackier and wackier through the years. Following are just a few real life examples I've collected.

A label on a baby stroller warns: *"Remove child before folding."*

A brass fishing lure with a three-pronged hook on the end warns: *"Harmful if swallowed."*

A flushable toilet brush warns: *"Do not use for personal hygiene."*

The label on a bottle of drain cleaner warns: *"If you do not understand, or cannot read, all directions, cautions and warnings, do not use this product."*

A cartridge for a laser printer warns, *"Do not EAT toner."*

A thirteen-inch wheel on a wheelbarrow warns: *"Not intended for highway use."*

A can of self-defense pepper spray alerts users, *"May irritate eyes."*

A snow blower cautions: *"Do not use snow blower on roof."*

A popular manufactured fireplace log warns: *"Caution— risk of fire."*

A dishwasher carries this warning: *"Do not allow children to play in the dishwasher."*

A household iron warns users: *"Never iron clothes while they are being worn."*

Or how about the one that just came out this year? This wins my "Wacky Warning Label of the Year" award. On a heat gun/paint remover that reaches a temperature of one thousand degrees: *"Do not use this tool as a hair dryer."*

Second place in this contest is a label the manufacturer placed on a kitchen knife, *"Never try to catch a falling knife."*

The following passage records how our first parents, Adam and Eve, ignored the one warning label in the whole world, were fatally injured, and had no one to blame but themselves.

Now the serpent was more cunning than any beast of the field which the LORD God had made. And he said to the woman, "Has God indeed said, 'You shall not eat of every tree of the garden'?"

And the woman said to the serpent, "We may eat the fruit of the trees of the garden; but of the fruit of the tree which is in the midst of the garden, God has said, 'You shall not eat it, nor shall you touch it, lest you die.'"

Then the serpent said to the woman, "You will not surely die. For God knows that in the day you eat of it your eyes will be opened, and you will be like God, knowing good and evil."

So when the woman saw that the tree was good for food, that it was pleasant to the eyes, and a tree desirable to make one wise, she took of its fruit and ate. She also gave to her husband with her, and he ate. Then the eyes of both of them were opened, and they knew that they were naked; and they sewed fig leaves together and made themselves coverings.

And they heard the sound of the LORD God walking in the garden in the cool of the day, and Adam and his wife hid themselves from the presence of the LORD God among the trees of the garden.

Then the LORD God called to Adam and said to him, "Where are you?" So he said, "I heard Your voice in the garden, and I was afraid because I was naked; and I hid myself."

And He said, "Who told you that you were naked? Have you eaten from the tree of which I commanded you that you should not eat?"

Then the man said, "The woman whom You gave to be with me, she gave me of the tree, and I ate."

And the LORD God said to the woman, "What is this you have done?" The woman said, "The serpent deceived me, and I ate." (Genesis 3:1-13)

This account of Satan's first temptation of the human race provides us with a wealth of information concerning his tactics.

tactics of the enemy

Here are three ploys Satan used to bring Eve to her fall:

1. he questioned GOD's word.

Satan didn't deny that God had spoken. He simply questioned whether God had really said what Eve *thought* He had said. He wanted her to think that perhaps she had misunderstood God's command. He wanted to "interpret" God's words for Eve. It's the same in our world today. Satan still twists the truth to try to alienate people from God.

2. he questioned GOD's love.

Satan wanted to make Eve think that God was holding something back. In reality, God Himself had placed this lone restriction in Adam and Eve's life to keep them from sinning. In the same way, the barriers God places in our lives are there because He loves us.

3. he substituted his own lie.

Satan led Eve to believe that if she ate of the tree she would become like God. At that point Eve had a choice: She could take God at His word, or believe Satan's lie.

Satan knows that our minds are "command central." This is where we reason, fantasize, and imagine. He will attempt to make you second-guess what God has said in His Word, or try to get you to dwell on the "what if's" in life.

Our counterattack is found in 2 Corinthians 10:4-5: "I use God's mighty weapons, not those made by men, to knock down the Devil's strongholds. These weapons can break down every proud argument against God and every wall that can be built to keep men from finding him." (NLT).

We see from this an important principle of satanic attack. Satan works from without to within, which is the very opposite of God's method. God begins His work in man's heart, with changes radiating outward that begin to effect his whole lifestyle. (If this isn't happening, it's questionable a true work of God has even begun).

Having eaten now of the "forbidden fruit," something unusual happens to Adam and Eve: "The eyes of both of them were opened" (v. 7).

the day everything changed

Sometimes "ignorance is bliss," and what Adam and Eve didn't know certainly didn't hurt them. Now their eyes are opened to the wickedness of sin, the deceitfulness of Satan, the weakness of their own nature, and the corruption that had wormed its way into God's perfect paradise.

It's sad to see a child lose his or her innocence—to be exposed to something corrupt, wicked, or depraved at an early age. In that sense, their eyes are opened. Far too often we know more about this wicked world than we need to know—and far less from the Word than we need to grow.

Paul wrote to the Romans: "I would have you well versed and wise as to what is good and innocent and guileless as to what is evil" (Romans 16:19, AMP). Now Adam and Eve had opened a "Pandora's box" that could never be closed again. Their eyes were opened to earth, but closed to heaven.

> And they heard the sound of the LORD God walking in the garden in the cool of the day. (Genesis 3:3)

This was normally a welcome event—the crowning moment of the whole day. But now they dreaded it because of their sin. When you are walking with God, you *love* fellowship with God and His people. His Word is attractive, and you find a strong desire to worship the Lord with other believers. But when you are in sin, you begin to dread the very things you used to love.

Note that it says, that the Lord came to them "in the cool of the day." What a beautiful picture that is, my favorite time of the day. The day has ended, but night has not yet fallen. The air begins to cool as the sun slips over the western horizon, bathing the world in a warm, golden light. Was this a special time that the Lord and Adam spent together each day? Perhaps the Lord even took some kind of human form to do this. If so, Adam must have greatly looked forward to it. (I would have!)

When something came up in the course of a day, Adam might have thought, "I must talk to the Lord about that this evening, in our time together." Perhaps some new discovery in the Garden he was commanded to tend had captured his imagination, and he could hardly wait to share his excitement with the Creator.

But now instead of looking forward to this daily event with joy, Adam deeply dreaded it.

GOD comes calling

It's interesting to note *when* God came to visit Adam and Eve. Not in the heat of the day—say, twelve noon, so Adam would think God was coming in the heat of passion. Not in the early morning, lest Adam think God couldn't wait to nail him for his sin. No, God came in the cool of the day. Loving, patient, grieved, yet demanding confession.

Adam had plenty of time to think about what he had done. The initial thrill of sin was gone. Now the guilt was kicking in, the remorse, the regret, that dead empty feeling that sin brings.

When God didn't find Adam waiting in their usual meeting place, He called out to him, "Adam, where are you?"

Why did God call out to Adam? Among other things, it was meant to reveal the deadly consequences of his sin. Often He needs to do that with us as well, because we have rationalized our sin in such a way that we don't even admit we've done it.

"Adam, Where are you?"

What tone of voice do you think God used?

"Adam! (You miserable failure!) Where are you?"

"Adam? (as in I can't find you) Where are you?"

I don't think it was either of the above. Rather, I believe there was hurt in that voice, but love as well, as a Father called out to His wayward son.

And there was Adam, the crown of God's creation, cowering behind a bush in fear. I can imagine God saying, "Well Adam, where has your sin taken you?"

What did God intend by asking Adam and Eve a series of questions in that terrible moment?

"Where are you?"

"Who told you that you were naked?"

"Have you eaten from the tree of which I commanded you that you should not eat?"

"What is this you have done?"

Obviously, God already knew the answers to those questions—in a deeper way than the man and woman could ever know them. It wasn't because God didn't know what was right and wrong, it was because He wanted to be sure that *they* knew it was wrong. He was looking for an admission of wrong-doing, an admission of sin. He desired nothing short of a full-blown confession.

God and His spokesmen in Scripture frequently asked questions to help people think through what they have just done.

Remember God with Elijah? *"What are you doing here?"*

Elisha with Gehazi: *"Where have you been?"*

Jesus to Judas *"Why have you come?"*

Instead of acknowledging his sin, however, Adam offers the mother of all excuses—in fact, it was the first recorded excuse in all of human history. "The woman who you gave to be with me…."

This shows the absolute wickedness of sin. Eve had been deceived—Scripture is clear on that.[2] But Adam, to his discredit and destruction, willfully and knowingly sinned. If that wasn't bad enough, he had the audacity to actually blame God for it! He was in essence saying, "*You* Lord, have sinned! This is *Your* doing. It's the woman *You* gave me! You're the one who brought Eve along!"

How easily God could have struck Adam down right where he stood. Like a spoiled little brat, he dared to suggest that it was God and not him who had failed. *God*, who had literally put him in paradise—with every possible comfort, surrounded by breath-taking beauty, such as has never been seen since. And yet in spite of all this, Adam lashed out at the very God who had provided so much for him. Jeremiah wrote, "Through the LORD's mercies we are not consumed, because His compassions fail not" (Lamentations 3:22).

That's what sin does. It blinds you to reality. And that's why we need God's provision for our forgiveness, so we can be restored into fellowship with Him.

God desires to walk with you in the cool of the day, just as He had enjoyed the company and fellowship of the first human beings. He wants to draw near to you, comfort you, instruct you, guide you, and lead you into a life of abundance and joy.

Could He be calling out to you right now, just as He called out to Adam?

Where are you?

Even as you begin this book—just a few pages in—you have the opportunity to respond to Him in a fresh way, to evaluate your life before His searching gaze.

Maybe it's time to ask yourself, *"Where am I? What am I doing here? How did I get to this place? Do I want to change?"* If so, you need to come to Jesus, asking His help to do that.

In the pages that follow, we'll be exploring some of the greatest true stories ever told on this world of ours. But *your* greatest story hinges on your relationship to your Creator and Savior, and allowing His life to flow through your life.

The cool of the day would be a good time to start.

But right now works, too.

chapter two

encounter east of eden: overcoming sin

d id you hear about the parrot in England that exposed a girl's sin?

This was a real news story, datelined, London, England.

A computer programmer found out his girlfriend was having an affair when his pet parrot kept repeating her lover's name, British media reported.

The African grey parrot kept squawking, "I love you, Gary" as his owner, Chris Taylor sat with girlfriend Suzy Collins on the sofa of their shared flat in Leeds, Northern England. When Taylor saw Collins' embarrassed reaction, he realized she had been having an affair, meeting her lover in the flat while Ziggy looked on.

Taylor said he had been forced to part with Ziggy after the bird continued to call out Gary's name, and refused to stop squawking the phrases in his ex-girlfriend's voice, media reports said.

"I wasn't sorry to see my old girlfriend Suzy go, after what she did, but it really broke my heart to let Ziggy go" he said. "I love him to bits and I really miss having him around, but it was torture hearing him repeat that name over and over again. I still can't believe he's gone, I know I'll get over Suzy, but I don't think Ill ever get over Ziggy."

You have to watch out for those parrots! In fact, the Bible warns all of us, *"You may be sure that your sin will find you out"* (Numbers 32:23, NLT). How will it happen? I can't tell you. It might even be through a parrot who becomes a stool pigeon!

We've all heard it said that man is basically good. In all of us, it is said, there's a desire to do the right thing, and it's only our upbringing, environment, or conditioning that makes us go bad.

I think it takes more faith to believe *that* than anything else I can think of. For if history tells us anything, it is that man is not good at all, but just the opposite. In fact, history as we know it is the story of the wars, intrigues, betrayals, injustice, destruction, and bloodshed of mankind.

But why? Why is this? Why has humanity throughout its entire history wrestled unendingly with this terrible problem of human hatred and bloodshed? Why are we at war with terrorists? Why the endless bloodshed in Iraq? Why the increasing tensions with North Korea and Iran?

If you want shallow, superficial answers to questions like these, you can find them in abundance. But Scripture teaches that the key to our Twenty-first century dilemma lies in a story of two brothers at the dawn of history.

the first family's tragedy

Now Adam knew Eve his wife, and she conceived and bore Cain, and said, "I have acquired a man from the LORD." Then she bore again, this time his brother Abel. Now Abel was a keeper of sheep, but Cain was a tiller of the ground. And in the process of time it came to pass that Cain brought an offering of the fruit of the ground to the LORD. Abel also brought of the firstborn of his flock and of their fat. And the LORD respected Abel and his offering, but He did not respect Cain and his offering. And Cain was very angry, and his countenance fell.

So the Lord said to Cain, "Why are you angry? And why has your countenance fallen? If you do well, will you not be accepted? And if you do not do well, sin lies at the door. And its desire is for you, but you should rule over it." (Genesis 4:1-7)

The story of the first family began happily enough. Adam and Eve conceived their first child. Neither the man nor woman had ever seen a human pregnancy before, much less a birth, so this was all new to them.

I was talking to a pastor friend of mine who was performing the wedding for his daughter. He wanted to say something really profound and moving as he was recounting her life. He began by saying to her and all the assembled guests, "I was there at your conception."

That was certainly assuring to hear! What he had meant to say was that he had been there at her *birth*.

Adam and Eve were present for both. One can only guess at Adam's amazement as he watched the changes in Eve.

"Eve, you seem to be putting on a lot of weight lately! What's with all these little socks you keep knitting? You want…what? Pickles and ice cream?"

After Adam had sinned with Eve in the Garden, God gave the very first messianic prediction.

"And I will put enmity
Between you and the woman,
And between your seed and her Seed;
He shall bruise your head,
And you shall bruise His heel."
(Genesis 3:15)

Isn't that just like our God? Even before He declared the consequences of their sin, He gave them a promise of ultimate deliverance and victory. You see that over and over in the prophetic portions of Scripture. There are plenty of warnings and pronouncements of judgment, but woven in and through these dark tidings are golden threads of hope and promise.

Adam and Eve, then, knew one was coming who would bruise Satan's head. Eve probably wondered, could this child in her womb be the one?

Finally the day came, and their firstborn arrived. They named him Cain, which means, *acquired*. In light of the promise of a Deliverer, the name might have meant, *"Here he is, I've gotten him."*

But tragically, Cain was not to be the Deliverer they hoped for…but a murderer instead. With the birth of the second child, a new and ominous element begins to enter the story.

playing favorites

Adam and Eve named their second son, Abel, which means "frail". This suggests that the physical effects of sin were already becoming apparent in the race. Regardless of whether this was physically true or not, it would certainly suggest a difference in the attitude of these parents toward their two boys. Cain was the strong one, the first born. Abel, weaker and more frail, was not as strong as Cain.

The names tell the story.

Son #1: Look, here comes ….Here he is!

Son #2: The weakling.

It would be very natural for them to favor Cain as the firstborn and the stronger of the two. "After all," they might have reasoned, "he may be the Deliverer God told us about." This strong hint of favoritism, found here at the beginning, may offer an insight into what was to follow.

If we follow this scenario, then the seeds of arrogance and pride had already been planted in Cain by his unsuspecting parents. We have to be so very careful as we raise our children to avoid favoritism at all costs. Later in Genesis, we see this same pattern in the way Isaac favored Esau, and Rebecca his wife favored Jacob. The favoritism drove a wedge between the two boys, setting into motion a conflict that followed them well into their adult years…and for many generations to come.

But did Jacob learn from those circumstances of his youth, bringing wisdom into his own parenting? Not a chance! Jacob so obviously favored his son Joseph that the young man became an object of hatred among his jealous brothers.

We must recognize that each child, though different, is a precious gift from God that we never, ever want to take for granted. They're not there for us to form into "our image," but rather for us to point them to God and help them to discover their God-given talents and abilities.

I read an article about this some time ago. It spoke of how parents, in their quest to raise happy, safe, and successful kids, go overboard in the praise department. They're called "helicopter parents," hovering over their kids and micromanaging their lives. They've bought into the myth that a child's self-esteem depends on never experiencing even the slightest adversity, upset, failure, or setback.

But this "no more tears" approach to raising kids is doing more harm than parents and teachers realize. "Of course we love our kids like crazy," says Betsy Hart, a Chicago-area mother of four and author of *It Takes a Parent.* "But when we idolize and idealize them, we're not doing them any favors. In fact, the result of these good intentions is often just the opposite. There's strong scientific evidence that undeserved praise can do long-term harm, especially when doled out to malleable teenagers. What's more, kids with a solution-minded parent constantly lurking don't develop the mettle to solve life's inevitable problems. So, by giving undeserved praise you can hurt a child's development."[3]

But then there's the problem of under-praising a child as well. A child who is never complimented or encouraged by his parents is bound for trouble! Did you know that by the time the average child enters kindergarten he has heard the word "No" over 40,000 times? If he is only told what is wrong with him and never right, he will soon lose hope and become convinced he's incapable of doing anything right. This false self-impression can carry through even into his adult years, and be passed on to his own children.

A child needs approval and encouragement in things that are good, every bit as much as he needs correction in things that are not.

I read about a young man named Antoine Fisher. A movie has been made about his life and how he rose from the worst of conditions. He was born in prison and sent to be raised in foster care. His father was killed by a girlfriend two months before Antoine was born. As the little boy grew, his foster mother tormented him with this singsong…..*You ain't nothing.*

You're never gonna be nothing, because you come from nothing.

What a wicked thing to say to a child. Antoine eventually proved her wrong, but this certainly made his journey that much harder. Make sure you let your kids know you love and value them today. It seems Adam and Eve over-favored Cain and under-favored Abel.

But even if Abel wasn't favored by his parents, he was favored by God! Those who are not favored by their parents often become the beloved of the Lord. With a gaping hole in their soul where the love of mom and dad should be, they turn to God with great desperation and desire.

And that's a good thing.

This was certainly the case with young David. You remember the story. When David's father Jesse understood that Samuel wanted to meet each of his sons, he paraded seven of his boys before the prophet. When Samuel said, "Is this all?", Jesse reluctantly called David in from the sheep pasture. And to the astonishment of everyone, the young shepherd was anointed as the next king of Israel.

It was so obvious—Jesse had little regard for his youngest son, and I can't imagine that the old sheep rancher spent much time with the boy. Perhaps because David's dad wasn't there for him when he needed a dad (we know little of his mother), the young man turned to God as a father.

In later years he wrote:

Even if my father and mother abandon me,
the LORD will hold me close.
(Psalm 27:10, NLT)

Do those words strike a chord in your heart? Perhaps that was your situation. You weren't favored by your parents. Maybe they divorced or never had time for you. But God is there as a heavenly Father for you, just as He willingly embraced David. He always has time for you, longs for your best, is more than willing to share His great wisdom and love, and will never fail or forsake you.

a tale of two offerings

The Bible tells us that a day came when Cain and Abel brought their offerings to God. "Here He Is" and "Weakling" brought the fruit of their labor before their Creator as a sacrifice. God accepted Abel's offering, but rejected Cain's.

Why?

Cain wasn't rejected because of his offering, but his offering was rejected because of Cain! The text makes it clear that Abel made his offering in the right way, and Cain did not.

Consider this: Cain and Abel were both raised in a godly home. Both heard the word of God from their youth, both of them were no doubt taught to pray and walk with God. But one of the boys grew up to be a true worshipper, offering an acceptable act of worship, while the other became a false worshipper, offering an unacceptable act of worship. One was accepted, the other rejected.

This reminds us that there is a right and wrong way to approach God. It all came down to the "why," or the motive. Because as far as God is concerned, motive is everything. The reason God accepted Abel's offering over Cain's is found in Hebrew 11:4.

> By faith Abel offered to God a more excellent sacrifice than Cain, through which he obtained witness that he was righteous, God testifying of his gifts; and through it he being dead still speaks.

"By faith Abel…." Adam and Eve's second-born exercised faith in his worship, Cain did not. Scripture reminds us "without faith it is impossible to please God." We must remember that worship is really a form of prayer. And the sad but amazing truth is that we can sing worship songs to God without a single thought of God while we're doing it!

Jesus once declared: "These people draw near to Me with their mouth, and honor Me with their lips, but their heart is far from Me. And in vain they worship Me, teaching as doctrines the commandments of men" (Matthew 15:8-9).

So there we are in a worship service, going through the motions. We sing the song. Maybe we lift our hands. But honoring God is really the farthest thing from our minds. As we drone on, we're really thinking, *I don't like this song…Look at the outfit that lady is wearing!…I'm kinda hungry. I wonder what I should have for lunch?…It's too cold in here…It's too hot in here…When is this service over?*

On any given Sunday, in any given worship service, we can look to our left and notice a man standing there with arms outstretched toward heaven, tears rolling down his cheeks, singing God's praises with a loud, clear, beautiful voice. *Look at that*, we say to ourselves. *Now that guy is really worshipping.*

Next to him might be a lady who has only raised her hands shoulder high, singing quietly (and not very well). And we find ourselves drawing a contrast, thinking, *She's not worshipping much at all.*

But what is worship? A lot of it comes down to what's happening within our hearts. There can be a place for outstretched arms as well as quiet voices. And as to the quality of the singing? Heaven couldn't care less!

Jesus told the story of a Pharisee and a tax collector who went to pray (or worship) at the temple.

> "The Pharisee stood and prayed thus with himself, 'God, I thank You that I am not like other men—extortioners, unjust, adulterers, or even as this tax collector. I fast twice a week; I give tithes of all that I possess.' And the tax collector, standing afar off, would not so much as raise his eyes to heaven, but beat his breast, saying, 'God, be merciful to me a sinner!' I tell you, this man went down to his house justified rather than the other; for everyone who exalts himself will be humbled, and he who humbles himself will be exalted." (Luke 18:11-14)

Those listening to the story were no doubt shocked by the way Jesus ended it. They were probably thinking Jesus would commend the Pharisee. But instead, He threw them a real curve ball.

"I tell you, this sinner, not the Pharisee, returned home forgiven!" (TLB)

Why did Jesus say such a thing? Because even though that religious leader may have lived an outwardly pure and devout life, inwardly his heart was full of pride.

And you cannot come into God's present with pride.

The apostle James tells us: "Humble yourselves in the sight of the Lord, and He shall lift you up" (James 4:10). Generations before those words were penned, the prophet Micah wrote:

> He has shown you, O man, what is good;
> And what does the Lord require of you
> But to do justly,
> To love mercy,
> And to walk humbly with your God?
> (Micah 6:8)

When we think of terrible sins against God, transgressions like adultery, stealing, and lying come to mind. And those sins certainly grieve His heart.

But so does pride.

In fact, the book of Proverbs underlines pride by listing it as one of the seven things God hates. By contrast, the distraught tax collector in the Lord's story saw himself for who he really was, praying, "God, be merciful to me a sinner."

a question and a warning

When Cain saw that God had accepted his brother's sacrifice and not his, he was angry. The Living Bible says "this made Cain both dejected and very angry, and his face grew dark with fury." Cain was hot. Seeing where this was headed, God lovingly reached out to the firstborn of humanity with a question.

The Lord said to Cain, "Why are you angry?"

With his over-the-top reaction to Abel's success, Cain began to show his true colors. Knowing Cain's heart, God was seeking to nip this murderous anger in the bud. Years before, as we read in the previous chapter, God had asked Cain's father an important question: "Adam, where are you?"

Instead of acknowledging what he had done, Adam replied, "I heard Your voice in the garden, and I was afraid because I was naked; and I hid myself" (Genesis 3:10).

Again, the Lord sought an admission of sin with a question. "Who told you that you were naked?" (v. 11)

And once again, instead of owning up to what he had done, Adam turned around and pointed a finger at Eve. "It's the woman you gave me!"

When God asked Cain, "Why are you angry?", what would the right answer have been? A humble admission of wrong. "Lord, I'm angry because I'm petty, sick with jealousy, and way off track. Please forgive me."

But Cain didn't respond to God at all. Just as his parents had done, he tried to cover up his sin instead of admitting his guilt. As they say, the apple doesn't fall far from the tree. Like father, like son. God wanted confession, because that is the way to forgiveness. There is no other way!

The Bible says, "If we confess our sins, He is faithful and just to forgive us our sins and to cleanse us from all unrighteousness. If we say that we have not sinned, we make Him a liar, and His word is not in us" (1 John 1:9-10).

God knew very well where this sin could lead, and He gave Cain a stern warning: "If you do well, will you not be accepted? And if you do not do well, sin lies at the door. And its desire is for you, but you should rule over it" (Genesis 4:7).

Sin lies at your door! In the original language the verse reads literally: *Sin is crouching at your door.* God could see it, like a crouching beast ready to tear Cain and his family apart. But Cain couldn't see it in that moment—or didn't want to see it.

Clearly Cain had not been doing well up to this point. But God, "who is not willing that any should perish," placed a stop sign—a red light—right in front of him. The Lord was saying, "If you don't heed this warning, you're flirting with disaster."

a lion at the door

It's no different today. Sin crouches at the door of every home, every office, every school, and even every church. It waits to attack and destroy the unwary. It is ever on the prowl, searching for the one it can take down.

A big game hunter named Peter H. Capstick wrote a chilling book called, *Death in the Long Grass.* The author tells one incredible story after another—not just on hunting lions, but on being hunted *by* lions.

After developing a taste for human blood, the huge cats would sneak into camp very late in the evening. Stepping over several men without waking them, the lions would choose their prey, and then drag them into the night. One large lion stalked and killed over a hundred men.

Charging lions can cover over 100 yards in just 3 seconds. The author wrote of keeping his ears open even as he slept in the camp, knowing that the lion would come swiftly and with deadly force.

It sounds like the picture of Satan that Peter used, doesn't it?

Be self-controlled and alert. Your enemy the Devil prowls around like a roaring lion looking for someone to devour. (1 Peter 5:8, NIV)

This is why we don't want to give the Devil any kind of foothold in our lives. And we don't want to let down our guard, either. Listen to this warning in Ephesians 4:26-27: "Don't sin by letting anger gain control over you. Don't let the sun go down while you are still angry, for anger gives a mighty foothold to the Devil" (NLT).

Sin is crouching at our doors, too! For some of us, it's already across the threshold. What that vulnerability might be will vary from person to person. But know this, just like that lion, the Devil is sizing up his prey, readying himself to strike!

But what can we do? How can we protect our homes from the power of Satan and his demon forces?

First of all, know this: *We cannot do it ourselves.*

Jesus drove that point home with this story: "When an evil spirit leaves a person, it goes into the desert, seeking rest but finding none. Then it says, 'I will return to the person I came from.' So it returns and finds its former home empty, swept, and clean. Then the spirit finds seven other spirits more evil than itself, and they all enter the person and live there. And so that person is worse off than before" (Matthew 12:43-45, NLT).

You might say this person was "repossessed."

The truth is, the victim went from bad to worse.

So what do we do when sin crouches at our door...when it seems to be creeping over the threshold and threatening our lives and our families? The only defense is Jesus Christ! When Satan knocks at my door I like to say, "Lord, would You mind getting that?"

Before a word is mentioned about what armor we are to wear into the spiritual battle, Ephesians 6 reminds us we are to "be strong in the Lord and in the power of His might" (v. 10).

If we are to master sin, we must first be mastered by Him who masters it! Tragically, Cain did not allow himself to be mastered by God, and so he became enslaved by the Devil.

my brother's keeper?

The Bible doesn't tell us what caused Cain to go so far as to murder his own brother. But I think it would be safe to say there was some jealousy and envy there, as he saw Abel's sacrifice accepted and his rejected.

Shakespeare called envy the "green-eyed monster." I heard the story of a crab fisherman who said he never needed a top for his crab basket. What kept them in their trap? He explained that if one of the crabs started to climb up the sides of the basket, the other crabs would reach up and pull it back down!

We can be a lot like those crabs, can't we? Though we would probably never admit it out loud, sometimes it bothers us to see others applauded, recognized, or rewarded. Cain allowed his jealousy and bitterness to get the best of him, and when he was overpowered, he struck out at his brother.

> Now Cain talked with Abel his brother; and it came to pass, when they were in the field, that Cain rose up against Abel his brother and killed him.

> Then the LORD said to Cain, "Where is Abel your brother?" He said, "I do not know. Am I my brother's keeper?" And He said, "What have you done? The voice of your brother's blood cries out to Me from the ground." (Genesis 4:8-10)

God had a couple more questions for Cain—very, very sad questions. *"Where is your brother?"* Cain bitterly responded, "How am I supposed to know? Am I my brother's keeper?"

What an evil reply. This is the first blatant lie. Cain knew perfectly well where his brother was…lying dead in the field. But sin had so completely mastered Cain that he not only lied, he lied to God. (No doubt thinking that he could get away with it.)

Whoever said sin made sense? How greatly sin had worked in just one generation. It was true that Adam and Eve, Cain's parents, tried to shift the blame when God confronted them with their sin. But they didn't lie. They told the truth even though they were desperately ashamed and trying to escape from under it.

But now, one generation later, Cain outright lies to God. And then he sets himself up to question God. *"Am I my brother's keeper?"*

This is even worse than the lie. He suggests that this brother, whom he just happened to kill, is not his responsibility. Cain is saying, "If something has happened to Abel, it's his own fault! Who knows…maybe he even deserved it."

God had given him fair warning, now Cain had to face the music.

> "So now you are cursed from the earth, which has opened its mouth to receive your brother's blood from your hand. When you till the ground, it shall no longer yield its

strength to you. A fugitive and a vagabond you shall be on the earth."

And Cain said to the LORD, "My punishment is greater than I can bear! Surely You have driven me out this day from the face of the ground; I shall be hidden from Your face; I shall be a fugitive and a vagabond on the earth, and it will happen that anyone who finds me will kill me."

And the LORD said to him, "Therefore, whoever kills Cain, vengeance shall be taken on him sevenfold." And the LORD set a mark on Cain, lest anyone finding him should kill him. Then Cain went out from the presence of the LORD and dwelt in the land of Nod on the east of Eden. (vv. 11-15)

Cain protested his punishment, but it's worth noting that he never repented of his sins. His words reveal remorse and regret... but no repentance.

We often confuse remorse and repentance. Remorse is being sorry for the *consequences* of your sin. Repentance is being sorry enough to stop doing it. Scripture says that "godly sorrow produces repentance." Cain was not repentant, he was simply sorry for the repercussions and results of sin in his life.

This is typical of the unrepentant person. Here they are, essentially reaping what they have sown, and they're angry with God for it! One of the clearest marks of sin is our almost innate desire to excuse ourselves and complain if we are judged in any way.

In our old nature, we don't like to admit our sin any more than Cain did.

voices from the grave

Hebrews 11 tells us that Abel, being dead, still speaks. From him, we learn a lesson of faith and presenting acceptable offerings to the living God. But Cain's life speaks, too. The Bible warns us that even today there is "the way of Cain."

Woe to them! For they have gone in the way of Cain.... (Jude 11)

What is this "way of Cain" Scripture warns of?

First, it is worshipping with impure motives. It doesn't matter how sacrificial your gift may be or how loudly you sing, if your heart is in the wrong place, it goes nowhere. The heart of the matter is the matter of the heart.

Second, the "way of Cain" is to allow your heart and life to become gripped by jealousy, envy, and hatred. There will always be people who will do better than you. They will have nicer things, larger ministries, closer families, better looks, and better health.

So what?

Hasn't God been good to you? Hasn't He done above and beyond what you could ask or think? Praise God if He has blessed or used someone besides yourself in a powerful way. Jealousy and envy are sins. And if left undealt with, they can become deadly. Remember the lion at the door!

Third, the way of Cain is to lie to God about what you have done, excusing your actions. *"Am I my brother's keeper?"* Do you think anything escapes the knowledge of our all-knowing Father?

In the book of Jeremiah, God asks a couple more very thought-provoking questions.

"Can anyone hide himself in secret places,
So I shall not see him?" says the LORD;
"Do I not fill heaven and earth?" says the LORD.
(Jeremiah 23:24)

There's no hiding from Almighty God. He calls on us to come out of our hiding places and come clean. He convicts us of our sin and even warns us of "sin crouching at our door." He speaks to us in many ways: through our personal devotions or a preacher or friend. We brush it off, rationalize it, and try all kinds of mental gymnastics to justify it. But deep down, we know the truth.

The shepherd has two primary tools he uses with sheep. David wrote: "Thy rod and thy staff, they comfort me" (Psalm 23:4, KJV).

The Lord will try to get your attention, using that staff. To switch metaphors, He will "fire one over the bow." Why does

God do this? Hebrews 12 tells us…

> For the Lord disciplines those he loves, and he punishes those he accepts as his children. As you endure this divine discipline, remember that God is treating you as his own children. Whoever heard of a child who was never disciplined? If God doesn't discipline you as he does all of his children, it means that you are illegitimate and are not really his children after all.

> For our earthly fathers disciplined us for a few years, doing the best they knew how. But God's discipline is always right and good for us because it means we will share in his holiness. No discipline is enjoyable while it is happening— it is painful! But afterward there will be a quiet harvest of right living for those who are trained in this way. (Hebrews 12:6-8, 10-11, NLT).

God warned Cain. But he just wouldn't listen. And the "way of Cain" led to a very unhappy end.

Don't walk that way! Don't follow Cain down the highway by letting jealousy and envy control and ruin your life. Don't let impure motives hinder your worship of God. Don't let sin master you!

Walk instead in the "way of Abel."

"It was by faith that Abel obeyed God and brought an offering that pleased God more than Cain's offering did. God accepted Abel and proved it by accepting his gift; and though Abel is long dead, we can still learn lessons from him about trusting God" (Hebrews 11:4, TLB).

Abel's way is the way of faith. It is the way of trust, the way of obedience, and the way of the cross.

In other words, it is the *only* way to life.

chapter three

encounter in canaan: making right choices

everyday of our lives, we are faced with literally hundreds of choices.

Walk into the door of your local supermarket. The very word "super" in front of "market" says it all. You can have a Super K-Mart on one corner, and a Wal-Mart Super Store on the other.

And talk about choices! In most such stores these days you'll find 24 different mixtures of bagged salads (organic or otherwise), a 107 varieties of cheese, 30 kinds of muffins, and 40 flavors of coffee. Stroll down the breakfast aisle and you'll encounter 80 brands of cereal—in the first ten feet!

Then you want to purchase a book? Go to Amazon.com for literally millions of titles—new or used. Break out the Ipod and you can play 20,000 songs, view 25,000 images, or watch 150 hours of video.

Slide into a booth at many restaurants and you'll find yourself confronted with a menu that's more like a small book. There are way too many choices!

Now what I eat or drink or what I wear probably won't have many long-lasting implications (except for having to let my clothes out because of the food I ate). But there are those significant, transforming choices we make in life. Like who we will marry. Or what career path we'll follow. Then there's the most important choice of all…the choice to follow Christ.

The pages of the Bible are filled with the stories of men and women who made choices that impacted the entire course of their lives.

—Moses chose to help his fellow Jews over the riches and power of Egypt.

—Joseph chose obedience to God over yielding
   to strong temptation.

—Daniel chose to eat kosher meals of vegetables over
   the unclean meat on the king of Babylon's banquet table.

Each one of these choices became major crossroads in the
lives of these individuals. What happened in those moments
of decision would set the course for the rest of their lives.

Moses, Joseph, and Daniel came to a dividing of the trails
and took the right paths. But what about those who made bad
choices at the parting of the ways? The Bible doesn't shy away
from describing the consequences.

Adam's choice cost him Paradise.

Esau's choice cost him his birthright.

Saul's choice cost him his kingdom.

Judas's choice cost him his apostleship, his life, and
his eternal soul.

Pilate, Agrippa, and Felix all chose wrong and missed eternity
with Christ.

As difficult as this idea may be to process, the choices we
make in time are binding in eternity. We make our decisions…
and then our decisions make us.

Yes, choices are incredibly important, as we will see in the
story before us.

excess baggage

God cares deeply about the choices we make in the course
of our lives. As human beings created in His image, we have
a free will, and both the ability and the responsibility to choose
our own destiny.

Because He loves us, God wants us to make decisions that
will lead us toward success and joy and fruitfulness in our lives
on earth, and then into His presence for eternity after we pass
from this life.

The Lord's heart for man and his choices can be summarized in Moses' heartfelt plea as the children of Israel stood on the brink of the Promised Land. Can you hear the heart of God ringing in these words?

> "Today I have given you the choice between life and death, between blessings and curses. I call on heaven and earth to witness the choice you make. Oh, that you would choose life, that you and your descendants might live! Choose to love the LORD your God and to obey him and commit yourself to him, for he is your life." (Deuteronomy 30:19-20, NLT)

In order to help and encourage us to choose life, the Bible gives us striking examples of those who chose well as well as those whose choices destroyed them. One such story details the choices of Abraham, and his nephew, Lot. Abraham made mostly right choices in life, while Lot made a series of wrong choices that he would live to bitterly regret.

Even though God will clearly show you the right choice to make, it's still up to *you* to decide. And you can't get around those moments of decision. Even when you have to make a choice and don't make it, that is in itself a choice!

God came one day to Abraham, then known as Abram, and told him to follow Him. He told him to make a clean break with his pagan family and follow.

Abram obeyed, but only partially. He had a very difficult time with this decision, and really "drug his feet." He also allowed his nephew Lot to tag along on the journey, something that the Lord really did not want him to do, and a decision that Abram no doubt regretted.

choose your companions with care

The Lord had said to Abram:

> "Get out of your country,
> From your family

And from your father's house,
To a land that I will show you."
(Genesis 12:1)

God was asking Abram to make a difficult separation in
his life. And He asks us to do the same. Why? Because we all
know people who both build us up or tear us down spiritually.
There are certain people who, after you've spent a few hours
with them, have actually diminished your spiritual appetite
and drawn you in the wrong direction. Sometimes these can
even be professing Christians who really don't have a heart
for spiritual growth. They're more interested in worldly things,
gossiping, complaining, or putting other people down.

The bottom line is they drag you down.

But then there are people who actually kindle a fire in your
heart for God. The more time you spend with them, the more
your spiritual appetite grows. They build you up in the faith
and make you want to be more like Jesus!

Paul told his young friend Timothy to "run from anything
that stimulates youthful lust. Follow anything that makes you
want to do right. Pursue faith and love and peace, and enjoy the
companionship of those who call on the Lord with pure hearts"
(2 Timothy 2:22, NLT).

This is not to say that we should avoid relationships with
nonbelievers. Not at all. Jesus wants us to seek to be a witness
to them. Paul told the church at Corinth:

When I wrote to you before, I told you not to associate with
people who indulge in sexual sin. But I wasn't talking about
unbelievers who indulge in sexual sin, or who are greedy or
are swindlers or idol worshipers. You would have to leave
this world to avoid people like that. What I meant was that
you are not to associate with anyone who claims to be a
Christian yet indulges in sexual sin, or is greedy, or worships idols, or is abusive, or a drunkard, or a swindler.
Don't even eat with such people. (1 Corinthians 5:9-11, NLT)

There's a difference between relationship and fellowship. I have relationships with people I come into contact with daily— neighbors, co-workers, extended family, and others. You can get to know the mailman who comes every day—and even have an extended conversation with him if you happen to bump into him in the mall. But that doesn't mean he's part of your inner circle of friends.

It's when you choose to spend time with someone that influence comes into play; you influence them and they influence you. And this is where we want to choose godly people to be our companions.

As we will see, Lot was not the kind of person God wanted Abe to hang with. They had different hearts, different priorities, different values. That's why He told Abram to separate from him.

Who was Lot? He was the son of Abram's brother, Haran, who remained back in the land of the Chaldeans when Abram went to Canaan. In the absence of his father, Lot may have looked to Abram to be that father figure in his life. There was something in Uncle Abraham that Lot so admired that he was willing to leave his country and immediate family to follow this man of God into the unknown.

That whole departure from their hometown of Ur is amazing when you think about it. Hebrews 11 tells us that "it was by faith that Abraham obeyed when God called him to leave home and go to another land that God would give him as his inheritance. *He went without knowing where he was going*" (vv. 8-9).

Can't you just hear their conversation?

"Where are you going, Uncle Abe?"

"I don't know, Lot. God hasn't told me yet."

"You don't know? You're pulling up stakes and leaving everything behind and you don't know where your even going?"

"That's right. That's the way it is."

"Oh…. Uncle Abe?

"Yes?"

"Can I come with you?"

Lot also chose to leave his community and all that was familiar. It wasn't because *he* had heard the voice of God, but simply because he admired and trusted his uncle.

Even so, it wouldn't be too long before a conflict developed…which led to a parting of the ways.

a parting of the ways

Then Abram went up from Egypt, he and his wife and all that he had, and Lot with him, to the South. Abram was very rich in livestock, in silver, and in gold. And he went on his journey from the South as far as Bethel, to the place where his tent had been at the beginning, between Bethel and Ai, to the place of the altar which he had made there at first. And there Abram called on the name of the LORD.

Lot also, who went with Abram, had flocks and herds and tents. Now the land was not able to support them, that they might dwell together, for their possessions were so great that they could not dwell together. And there was strife between the herdsmen of Abram's livestock and the herds-men of Lot's livestock. The Canaanites and the Perizzites then dwelt in the land.

So Abram said to Lot, "Please let there be no strife between you and me, and between my herdsmen and your herdsmen; for we are brethren. Is not the whole land before you? Please separate from me. If you take the left, then I will go to the right; or, if you go to the right, then I will go to the left."

And Lot lifted his eyes and saw all the plain of Jordan, that it was well watered everywhere (before the LORD destroyed Sodom and Gomorrah) like the garden of the LORD, like the land of Egypt as you go toward Zoar. Then Lot chose for himself all the plain of Jordan, and Lot journeyed east. And they separated from each other. Abram dwelt in the land of Canaan, and Lot dwelt in the cities of the plain and pitched his tent even as far as Sodom. But the men of Sodom were exceedingly wicked and sinful against the LORD. (Genesis 13:1-13)

During their journey through Canaan, Abraham and Lot had each acquired great wealth. By this time, Lot was feeling pretty good about his decision to latch onto his uncle. Abraham's prosperity seemed to have an overflow into his nephew's pockets.

Prosperity, of course, isn't necessarily bad or good. It all depends on how it affects a person. Over the course of time, a conflict developed between those that kept the flocks for Abraham and Lot. In reality, however, the problem between Abraham and Lot wasn't caused by the land, the famine, their wealth, or even their herdsmen.

The heart of every problem is the problem in the heart.

Lot's heart was centered on wealth and worldly achievement, while Abraham wanted only to please the Lord. Abraham acquired wealth along the way, but it never became important to him. For Lot, however, the wealth and the prestige it brought became his reason for living. These two men had walked together for a time, but eventually a friction developed because of the spiritual direction each had chosen to go in life.

The Bible asks, "Can two walk together, except they be agreed?" (Amos 3:3). Abraham was a man who wanted to walk closely with God and enjoy fellowship with Him. In contrast, Lot wanted a friendship with God like his uncle had—but he also wanted friendship with the world.

The Bible clearly warns against this sort of divided allegiance. The apostle James wrote: "You adulterers! Don't you realize that friendship with this world makes you an enemy of God? I say it again, that if your aim is to enjoy this world, you can't be a friend of God" (James 4:4).

But Lot wanted to have it both ways. He had a knowledge of God and knew what was right, but he was weak. He didn't want to make a stand, and tended to lean on Abraham for strength.

Abraham walked with God…and Lot walked with Abraham! There are many like Lot today: They know what is right and deep-down want to know God. But there is a weakness in their faith and character. They need other believers to constantly prop them up, or they will fall. At the same time, they have a fascination with this world, and flirt on the edges on sin.

Interestingly enough, these are often people who have been raised in church.

For those who have already tried what this world offers, that attraction isn't nearly so strong. *Been there, done that, bought the T-shirt.* In Luke 7:47, Jesus said, "A person who is forgiven little shows only little love." But when you've never "been there or done that" you can take your spiritual heritage for granted.

This is what Lot was doing, hoping he could ride along on his uncle's spiritual coattails. But it didn't work. In fact, it never works. We can't live off of someone else's faith. God has no grandchildren. The thing that kept Abraham from sin was his friendship with God—walking with God, talking with God, enjoying His presence. It was that love for the Lord that kept everything else in perspective. When you know and love God and see Him for who He is, you will also see this world for what it is.

leaving the results to GOD

The day finally came for Lot and Abraham to separate. Friction between the herdsmen was the surface reason—but it really went much deeper than that, to a basic difference in focus and purpose. Lot was at war with Abraham because he was at war with himself. And he was at war with himself because he was at war with God.

Abraham, however, was determined to be a peacemaker, and generously gave Lot his choice of territory. By not choosing for himself, Abraham was making a profound choice. He had decided to put God first and simply trust Him to take care of him and his family.

"Is not the whole land before you? Please separate from me. If you take the left, then I will go to the right; or, if you go to the right, then I will go to the left" (Genesis 13:9).

By not choosing for himself, Abraham chose to leave the outcome up to God. "You go ahead, Lot," he says. "I'll be fine whichever way it goes." Abraham felt that if he had to give up anything in the process, it really didn't matter. What mattered was obedience to God and His word.

Do you find yourself in a similar situation right now?

Maybe you're afraid that if you are honest and forthright in business, that lying cheat of a competitor will take advantage of you and steal away your customers. And that's exactly what might happen. You very well might lose some ground. But what's more important, the fast buck or the smile of God?

Maybe you're apprehensive that if you're are upfront with some of your friends about your faith in Christ and the convictions you hold as a result of that faith, they'll walk away from you. They may. But what's more important, friendship with God or friendship with this world?

Maybe you're living with your boyfriend or girlfriend outside of marriage. You can't separate, you say, because it would be so much more expensive. You couldn't afford to do it. The truth is, you can't afford *not* to do it. At the end of the day, the will of God is all that matters.

We, like Abraham, must face tough choices. Will we opt for the easy way and make the choice that pleases ourselves, or will we take the more difficult path of obedience, and leave the results up to God?

Lot made the wrong choice, opting for what looked to be the better land—not realizing the hidden costs that would be assessed against his family.

As it turned out, it was much, much more than he could afford.

downward steps

Lot took a long look at the fertile plains of the Jordan Valley in the direction of Zoar. The whole area was well watered everywhere, like the garden of the LORD or the beautiful land of Egypt. (This was before the LORD had destroyed Sodom and Gomorrah.) Lot chose that land for himself — the Jordan Valley to the east of them. He went there with his flocks and servants and parted company with his uncle Abram. (Genesis 13:10-11, NLT)

There were a series of steps that led to the situation in which Lot ultimately found himself. Whenever we end up in sin, it's always the cumulative product of small indulgences and seemingly minuscule compromises. The immediate consequences of those actions, at the time, seem almost indiscernible.

So what did Lot do wrong?

first step down: he looked the wrong way.

And Lot lifted his eyes and saw all the plain of Jordan, that it was well watered everywhere…like the land of Egypt. (v. 10)

Lot's point of reference was Egypt. He liked Sodom because it reminded him of Egypt. What is your point of reference?

My wife tells me that I always compare every place I go to Hawaii. I lived there in my childhood, and have visited many times since. The Hawaiian Islands have always held a special place in my heart.

So whenever we are visiting someplace that has a tropical feel to it, I might say, "Well, this is nice. But not as nice as Hawaii!" Or maybe, "This reminds of a place in Hawaii."

Lot's point of reference was Egypt.

He looked around at the land, caught sight of Sodom and Gomorrah, and made his first step down. The wording in the original language reveals that Lot "looked with longing" on that well-watered plain.

This reminds us of what happened to Eve. "So when the woman saw that the tree was good for food, that it was pleasant to the eyes, and a tree desirable to make one wise, she took of its fruit and ate" (Genesis 3:6).

The apostle John made a strong statement about that long look in the wrong direction:

> For all that is in the world—the lust of the flesh, the lust of the eyes, and the pride of life—is not of the Father but is of the world. And the world is passing away, and the lust of it; but he who does the will of God abides forever. (1 John 2:16-17)

Instead of lifting up his eyes to heaven, Lot lifted up his eyes to the plain of Jordan and stopped there. The eyes see what the heart loves. Abraham had taken Lot out of Egypt, but he could not take Egypt out of Lot.

Our outlook helps to determine our outcome. Abraham walked by faith, and Lot walked by sight.

second step down:
he separated himself from abraham

Separation may have been a good thing for Abraham, who had his own walk with the living God. But it was disastrous for Lot, who didn't have that kind of heart-tie to the Lord. A sure sign of spiritual decline is when we find ourselves wanting to get away from godly people, preferring the company of friends and the activities that "remind us of Egypt." For instance, we attach a token prayer to the beginning or the end of an otherwise completely godless evening, and imagine we have spiritually "sanitized" everything.

third step down:
he pitched his tent toward sodom (genesis 13:12).

What was it that so fascinated Lot about the two evil cities on the plain? The music? The bright lights? The urban sophistication? The flashy chariots? The freewheeling lifestyle? The Bible doesn't tell us what became such a drawing card for Abraham's nephew. We only know that he edged closer and closer, imagining that he could still keep his faith and character, and that he could "handle" any temptations that came his way.

If you had asked Lot why, at this time of his life, he settled near Sodom but didn't actually go and live in the city, he might have explained to you that Sodom was a very wicked place. At the same time, however, there were certain advantages to living nearby.

I've spoken to many people like this through the years. They don't want to plunge whole-hog into a pagan lifestyle…but they don't completely walk away from it, either. They want to be close enough to the world to still "keep an eye on it," but not actually participate in it.

At heart, Lot was still a righteous man, as Peter tells us in the New Testament. He writes that Lot "was oppressed by the filthy conduct of the wicked," and that it "tormented his righteous soul from day to day by seeing and hearing their lawless deeds" (2 Peter 2:7, 8). So before the man and his family became completely swallowed by the evil of that place, God sent a strong warning.

In an interesting turn, Lot was captured by an alliance of kings who had made war on Sodom and its allies and defeated them. Raiding the city of Sodom, the invaders took Lot as a hostage and marched away. Surely this was a warning to Lot from God that he was moving in the wrong direction!

Have you ever had a "wake-up call" from heaven, where you distinctly sensed God warning you about something? Lot probably cried out to God, "O Lord, if You get me out of this, I'll serve You! I'll be Your friend like Uncle Abraham. I'll stay away from Sodom!"

God doesn't want us to fall or fail. And He will send us warnings about our direction, beginning with our conscience. That little "warning buzzer" goes off when you start to cross the line…and what do you do with it? Ignore it? Shut it out with lots of noise and activities? Do you try to disable it, like pulling the battery out of a smoke alarm?

Besides the voice of our conscience, God will set obstacles to our path. For Balaam, it was an angel in the middle of the road—and a talking donkey. For Jonah, it was a great fish with an appetite for runaway prophets. For Peter, it was a servant girl who identified him while he stood by the enemy's fire. But even in the face of such obstacles we may persist in our stubborn way.

Maybe God is warning you right now. That relationship with that co-worker of the opposite sex is getting a little too close. Those lunches together, those e-mails, instant messages, and phone calls. That habit you have of "stretching the truth" when asked about some of your actions. And then you have to tell another lie to cover up the one you previously told. Deep down, you know you're flirting with disaster. Stop! Before it's too late. You don't want to end up like Lot!

Uncle Abraham bravely led an attack and saved his compromising nephew. And how did Lot show his gratitude to God? He pulled up stakes and moved right into Sodom!

fourth step down:
he sat in the gateway of sodom (genesis 19:1)

Sitting in the gateway means he had actually become one of the leaders in this wicked and perverse city. I wonder what kind of compromises he had to make to pull this off? Graham Scroggie once said of compromise: "It prompts us to be silent when we ought to speak for fear of offending. It prompts us to praise when it is not deserved to keep people our friends. It prompts us to tolerate sin and not to speak out because to do so might give us enemies."

How important it is for us to realize that compromise reaches no one. If it causes us to lower our standards in order to extend our reach, we have defeated our very purpose. In Lot's case, it led him to the leadership of a city he should have been calling into account. Like a moth attracted to a flame, Lot had been unable to keep his distance—and now he was in the very place God was about to destroy. By this time, Lot had become so spiritually dull he didn't even realize how bad things had become. Sin had worn him down.

Jesus told us that as Christians in this world, we are to be both salt and light. Some are salt but not light (they live it but they don't share it). Others are light but not salt (they share it but they don't live it). It appears that Lot was neither.

But in all fairness, Lot is not a prototype of a non-believer pretending to be one. Rather, he is a picture of a believer living a compromised life.

Remember the word about this unhappy man in 2 Peter? Lot was "a good man who was sick of all the immorality and wickedness around him" (2:7, NLT).

Poor Lot. He was so worn down spiritually he didn't seem to know which way was up. So what did Uncle Abraham do? Did he "pile on" and condemn Lot? No, he prayed. And that's exactly what God would have us do for those who have compromised their faith and fallen onto hard times. They need to see this for themselves, and God can bring that about through the conviction of His Holy Spirit.

Out of regard for Abraham—and mercy for Lot—God sent two angels to literally take Lot and his family by the hand and pull them out of that perverse place before the judgment of God fell. I see two powerful realities at work in that rescue: the incomparable mercy of God and the mighty power of prayer.

abraham's choice

Let's go back to that destiny-making moment when Abraham and Lot stood on that high ridge overlooking the plain of the Jordan. Abraham seemingly left the choice up to Lot, as to which direction the younger man would go—but he actually left the matter with God.

After Lot went off toward what would become a bitter future in the lush fields surrounding Sodom and Gomorrah, the word of the Lord came to Abraham with a stunning promise.

And the LORD said to Abram, after Lot had separated from him: "Lift your eyes now and look from the place where

you are — northward, southward, eastward, and westward;
for all the land which you see I give to you and your descendants forever. And I will make your descendants as
the dust of the earth; so that if a man could number the
dust of the earth, then your descendants also could be
numbered. Arise, walk in the land through its length
and its width, for I give it to you."

Then Abram moved his tent, and went and dwelt by
the terebinth trees of Mamre, which are in Hebron,
and built an altar there to the LORD. (Genesis 13:14-18)

You don't lose when you choose God. You might not look
like a winner in the world's eyes, and your life may have its share
of hardships and sorrows. But God knows how to reward His
own, and He is a generous Father. We hear the phrase "treasure
in heaven" and picture something in earthly terms, like a big
chest of gold or diamonds. But we really don't have a clue how
majestic and awesome and incredibly joyous God's rewards
will be for His faithful children.

When I think about these things, I remember how
Peter reminded the Lord of the sacrifice he and his fellow
disciples had made.

"We have left everything to follow you! What then will
there be for us?"

Jesus said to them… "Everyone who has left houses or
brothers or sisters or father or mother or children or fields
for my sake will receive a hundred times as much and will
inherit eternal life." (Matthew 19:27, 29, NIV)

This saying is vividly illustrated here in Abraham's life. He
had now given up everything to follow God—not only his own
country and people but now some prime real estate in Canaan,
giving Lot first choice in the matter. Not only that, but he had
lost Lot, too, for whom he had some real affection.

Lot had lifted up his eyes and seen what the world had to offer. So God said to Abraham, "Lift up your eyes and see all I have given you." Had Abraham lost the best land? Well, in its place God was giving him the entire land of Canaan. He was to have it all. Had Abraham lost family for the sake of obedience? Now God would give to him offspring like the dust of the earth.

We all choose what path our life will take. God always gives His very best to those who leave the choice with Him.

This reminds me of the tragic pioneer story of the Donner Party. It took place in high Sierra Nevadas in the winter of 1846. George and Jacob Donner, James Frazier Reed, and their families packed up everything to head for the "Promised Land" in California, some 2,000 miles away. Their caravan had state of the art covered wagons laden with more than enough supplies. By the time they set out, their party had swelled to 87 men, women, and children.

Their journey ended in tragedy, however, when forced to camp for the winter at a small lake about 13 miles northwest of Lake Tahoe. There they suffered heavy snows—and the deaths of forty of their company. Some of the others, desperate to survive, turned to cannibalism. That aspect of the story of the Donner party is well known. What is not so well known is how they ended up in this miserable place.

A man named Lansord Hastings had told them he knew of a shortcut to California. Though it was untried, the Donner party took it. And it cost them everything. One wrong foolish, impetuous decision resulted in disaster.

Perhaps you, like the Donner Party, find yourself at a cross-roads in your life. You know the right way to go, but then…there's that shortcut that looks so tempting. Abraham made the right choices, and lived the right way. Lot made the wrong choice, and to a large degree, lived the wrong way.

As Elijah said to the faithless people of Israel up on Mount Carmel: "How long are you going to waver between two opinions? …If the Lord is God, *follow* him! But if Baal is God, then follow *him!*" (1 Kings 18:21, TLB).

You know what is right. Don't take the shortcut of Lot. Walk in the right way like Abraham.

Having lived 54 years now, I have the perspective of viewing several generations: my grandparents' generation, my parents' generation, my generation that is still unfolding, my children's generation, and my grandchildren's generation, that is just beginning. It's sobering to see how choices made by one generation can have a ripple effect for decades to come…bringing either life, peace, and prosperity, or sorrow and brokenness.

As I said, the choices of time are binding in eternity. Contrast two men from the Nineteenth Century: Max Jukes and Jonathan Edwards.

Max Jukes lived in New York. He did not believe in Christ or in raising his children in the way of the Lord. He refused to take his children to church, even when they asked to go. Since he walked this planet, Max Jukes has had 1,026 descendants. Of this number, 300 were sent to prison for an average term of thirteen years; 190 were public prostitutes; 680 were admitted alcoholics. The descendants of this man made no contribution whatsoever to society.

Jonathan Edwards lived in the same state, at the same time as Jukes. Edwards, however, loved the Lord and saw that his children were in church every Sunday, as he served the Lord to the best of his ability. He has had 929 descendants, and of these 430 were ministers, 86 became university professors, 13 became university presidents, 75 authored good books, 7 were elected to the United States Congress, and one was Vice President of the United States.

Choices! We all make them. Hundreds every day. To whom do you relate most in this message: Abraham or Lot? Are you a "friend of God" or a "friend of this world"?

chapter four

encounter in haran: knowing the will of GOD

oes God still speak to man today?
Is He interested in what happens to us as individuals?
Does He truly have a master plan for our lives?

If so, how do I discover it? How do I hear His voice? How can I know the will of God?

These are all important questions, and the answer to the first one sets us an exciting journey of discovery. *Yes.* God does speak to man today—and especially to His own sons and daughters. We as Christians are not simply victims of chance in a random world, hoping against hope our luck won't run out on us. Just as God led men and women in the pages of Scripture, so He wants to lead us. There are, however, no foolproof formulas or easy 1-2-3 steps we can follow that will instantaneously reveal God's will to us at our every whim.

But let there be no doubt: God guides His own. The gospel of John tells us that Jesus "calls his own sheep by name and leads them out. And when he brings out his own sheep, he goes before them; and the sheep follow him, for they know his voice" (John 10:3-4).

God speaks to us and shows us His will—in terms both general and specific—and in the next few pages we will examine some of the foundational principles of His guidance in our daily lives.

The good news is that God does not play hide and seek with us. *He wants to lead you even more than you want to be led.* God is more concerned about keeping us in His will than we are to be kept in it!

his will is best

Far too often, we can make knowing God's will into something misty, mystical, and other-worldly. And yet through my years of walking with God, I have found that there are concrete, practical steps we as believers can take to more easily grasp and understand His will.

God's way becomes plain when we start walking in it. But sometimes we fear or don't like His plan, and don't want to follow it. The following is a reported transcript of a conversation between the captain of a US Navy ship with Canadian authorities off the coast of Newfoundland.

Canadians: Please divert your course 15 degrees to the south to avoid a collision.

Americans: Recommend you divert your course 15 degrees to the north to avoid a collision.

Canadians: Negative. You will have to divert your course 15 degrees to the south to avoid a collision.

Americans: This is the captain of a US Navy ship. I say again, divert your course!

Canadians: No. I say again, you divert your course.

Americans: This is the aircraft carrier USS Lincoln, the second largest ship in the United States Atlantic fleet. We are accompanied by 3 destroyers, 3 cruisers and numerous support vessels. I demand that you change your course 15 degrees north. I say again, that's one five degrees north, or counter measures will be undertaken to ensure the safety of this ship.

Canadians: This is a lighthouse. Your call!

Often we're just like that Navy captain when it comes to the will of God. We want Him to divert His course, when we're in desperate need of diverting our own. Above all else, however, we should keep one important fact in mind: In the long run,

God's will is *always* better than our will.

In the long run?

The reality is, at certain times in our lives we may not understand or even like God's will. If you were to interview young Joseph, deep in the bowels of an Egyptian prison on a trumped up rape charge (Genesis 39-40), he may have not been all that excited about the will of God for his life. But if you were to talk to him just a short time later, after he came into power as the second in command of Egypt, he might have preached a sermon to you about the value of waiting for God's will.

Keep this in mind. God is always looking out for your spiritual and eternal welfare. We tend to look out for our physical and immediate welfare. But what is good *now* may not be for eternity. And what is difficult now may be the best thing for the endless ages to come.

Paul wrote these encouraging words to the church in Corinth:

> For our present troubles are quite small and won't last very long. Yet they produce for us an immeasurably great glory that will last forever! So we don't look at the troubles we can see right now; rather, we look forward to what we have not yet seen. For the troubles we see will soon be over, but the joys to come will last forever. (2 Corinthians 4:17-18, NLT)

The story before us in this chapter uncovers several essential principles for knowing the will of God in our life. It also happens to be a beautiful love story—on two levels. First, it's the story of a man and woman who come together against almost impossible odds, all because of the providence of God. Second, it's a picture or type of God's love for each of us, how He sought us out and graciously brought us to Himself.

matchmaker, matchmaker

When the patriarch Abraham was an old man, at this point pushing 140 years, his miracle son Isaac was about 40. Sarah, Isaac's mother, had died, and Isaac was lonely and heartsick.

Abraham may have been old, but there was nothing wrong with his intellectual powers.

It didn't take him long to figure out what his son needed. Isaac needed a wife.

Hard as it might be to imagine, there weren't any Internet matchmaking sites in those days, so Abraham called his most trusted servant, and gave him some specific instructions.

> Abraham said to the oldest servant of his house, who ruled over all that he had, "Please, put your hand under my thigh, and I will make you swear by the LORD, the God of heaven and the God of the earth, that you will not take a wife for my son from the daughters of the Canaanites, among whom I dwell; but you shall go to my country and to my family, and take a wife for my son Isaac."

> And the servant said to him, "Perhaps the woman will not be willing to follow me to this land. Must I take your son back to the land from which you came?"

> But Abraham said to him, "Beware that you do not take my son back there. The LORD God of heaven, who took me from my father's house and from the land of my family, and who spoke to me and swore to me, saying, 'To your descendants I give this land,' He will send His angel before you, and you shall take a wife for my son from there. And if the woman is not willing to follow you, then you will be released from this oath; only do not take my son back there." So the servant put his hand under the thigh of Abraham his master, and swore to him concerning this matter.

> Then the servant took ten of his master's camels and departed, for all his master's goods were in his hand. And he arose and went to Mesopotamia, to the city of Nahor. (Genesis 24:2-10)

As the servant, Eliezer, arrived at his destination, he shot a quick prayer heavenward and asked God for direction and success in his mission. This is the privilege of a man or woman who enjoys a moment-by-moment walk with God. Scripture tells us to "pray without ceasing" (1 Thessalonians 5:17). That doesn't mean we're to be on our knees 24/7, but it does mean staying tuned into heaven's frequency every waking hour of our day. Then, when the road forks in front of us, when a sudden need arises in our lives, we can launch a swift "arrow" prayer toward heaven, confident that God is watching and that He will hear us.

That's what Eliezer did. When he saw some young women approaching the well where he stood with his mini-caravan, he prayed that the one whom God had chosen for Isaac would not only offer him a drink of water (a common courtesy), but also offer to water his camels (a great inconvenience).

Before he had finished his prayer, a gorgeous young woman named Rebekah approached the well. *(Lord, let her be the one! Let her be the one!)* As she was drawing water, Eliezer asked her for a drink. She graciously complied, and then offered to get water for his camels until their considerable thirst was completely satisfied.

Don't minimize that act of courtesy. Watering these animals was no small feat when you consider the fact that an average camel drinks more than 20 gallons of water—especially after a long day's journey through the desert. And Eliezer had 10 camels with him. You do the math…that's a lot of water to be hauled up from a well with a bucket.

In fact, if Rebekah's pitcher held a gallon, that meant she would have had to make 200 trips from the spring to the watering trough. At the least, it would have involved several hours of labor. And remember, at that point Rebekah had no idea who this stranger was. She had no clue about a wealthy and godly eligible bachelor named Isaac waiting many miles away. She simply saw a stranger in need and took it upon herself to help him.

Eliezer was overjoyed, and immediately pulled out a ring and some bracelets from his bag, asking the surprised Rebekah who her family was and if he could meet them. When Rebekah arrived at the family tent, bedecked with beautiful jewelry,

followed by a distinguished stranger, and with ten camels
in tow, she definitely had her brother Laban's attention.

When the young woman told Laban the story, he was all
smiles. Opening his arms in welcome, he declared, "Come in,
O blessed of the LORD! Why do you stand outside? For I have
prepared the house, and a place for the camels" (Genesis 24:31).
Laban must have been expecting company!

Eliezer, however, wasted no time in declaring his mission. At
the request of Abraham, he had come seeking a bride for his master Isaac. Then he related the story of his prayer at the well, and
what Rebekah had done. Rebekah's family couldn't deny the evi-
dent hand of God in these developments, and they agreed to her
going back with Eliezer to be the bride of Isaac. Realizing they
would probably never see her again, they asked if she could wait
awhile, allowing them to say a long goodbye. But Eliezer knew he
was on God's business, and said no, she must leave immediately.

> So they said, "We will call the young woman
> and ask her personally."
>
> Then they called Rebekah and said to her,
> "Will you go with this man?"
>
> And she said, "I will go."
> (Genesis 24:58)

1. search the scriptures for GOD's general will

The first principle of laying hold of God's will is that you must
look for it. And the best and primary place to being your search
is in the pages of Scripture. When this story unfolded, nothing approaching Scripture as we have it today existed. But the
principles of biblical truth already existed, being passed on orally
from generation to generation. In this situation, God's word came
through the lips of Abraham.

> "The LORD God of heaven, who took me from my father's
> house and from the land of my family, and who spoke to
> me and swore to me, saying, 'To your descendants I give

this land,' He will send His angel before you, and you shall take a wife for my son from there." (Genesis 24:7)

Abraham also added that this wife for Isaac was not to come from the pagan Canaanites. She was to be of his extended family, which was the equivalent of being a believer at this time.

Today, God speaks to us through His Word. That is the bedrock of truth by which we measure all other truth, the clear revelation by which we measure all other so-called revelations. It is the rock of stability by which we measure our fickle human emotions. The way we know something is true or right is by comparing it to what Scripture teaches.

Everything you need to know about God is found in the pages of Scripture. Paul told his young disciple Timothy that "All Scripture is inspired by God and is useful to teach us what is true and to make us realize what is wrong in our lives. It straightens us out and teaches us to do what is right. It is God's way of preparing us in every way, fully equipped for every good thing God wants us to do" (2 Timothy 3:16, NLT).

From this verse—and others like it—we know that God would never lead us contrary to the plain teachings of Scripture. This truth seems obvious (and it is), but it's amazing how many seem to miss it. They're busy seeking some mystical word from God when He has plainly spoken to them in the Bible sitting on their nightstand.

It would be like wanting desperately to hear from someone that you deeply loved. Then one day you looked in your mailbox and found a letter from them. (Or an e-mail on your computer.) But instead of opening that piece of correspondence, you simply continued to whine about how this person never communicates with you.

Don't be ridiculous…open the letter!

In the same way we must open The Book! Jesus said, "Behold, I have come—in the volume of the book it is written of Me—to do Your will, O God" (Hebrews 10:7).

Whenever you begin to imagine that the will of God is mysterious, mystical, or out-of-reach, remember that Scripture plainly states God's specific will for you—again and again. Are you looking for God's will but don't know where to begin? Start with what God has already told you. If you're not ready to obey His clearly written instructions, what makes you think you will follow special revelation out of the blue?

> *For this is the will of God*, your sanctification: that you should abstain from sexual immorality. (1 Thessalonians 4:3)

> Rejoice always, pray without ceasing, in everything give thanks; *for this is the will of God in Christ Jesus for you.* (1 Thessalonians 5:16-18)

Therefore do not be unwise, *but understand what the will of the Lord is.* And do not be drunk with wine, in which is dissipation; but be filled with the Spirit, speaking to one another in psalms and hymns and spiritual songs, singing and making melody in your heart to the Lord, giving thanks always for all things to God the Father in the name of our Lord Jesus Christ, submitting to one another in the fear of God. (Ephesians 5:17-21)

2. ask for GOD's specific will

When I was a young man, I never found any specific passage in Scripture that told me I must marry a girl named Cathe. What do I do, then? I take God's principles, keeping them in the forefront of my mind and heart, and then ask Him for His specific will in my life. From the Scripture, I understand that it's not good for a man to be alone, that an excellent wife is the crown of her husband, and that he who finds a wife finds a good thing, and obtains favor from the Lord. Not to mention the verse that says it's better to marry than to burn with passion![4]

Having understood God's general will for my life through the Scriptures, I seek His specific will for individual situations as they arise.

This is what Eliezir did.

Then he said, "O LORD God of my master Abraham, please give me success this day, and show kindness to my master Abraham." (Genesis 24:12)

Nothing is too insignificant, too minute, to take to the Lord in prayer. There's an old Jewish proverb that says, "It is better to ask the way ten times than to take the wrong road once." The apostle James reminds us, "If you need wisdom—if you want to know what God wants you to do—ask him, and he will gladly tell you. He will not resent your asking" (James 1:5, NLT).

3. wait for his timing

The timing of God is just as important as the will of God. And it is clear that God has both His perfect will and time to do what He wants. Ecclesiastes 3:11 tells us that "He has made everything beautiful in its time."

Eliezir waited for the right moment to act. He saw the beautiful Rebekah, and hoped she might be the one.

And the man, wondering at her, remained silent so as to know whether the LORD had made his journey prosperous or not. (Genesis 24:21)

The problem with so many of us is that having found God's will, we want to act quickly. Eliezir waited to see if this was indeed the one. The Lord answered his prayer, Rebekah responded, and Eliezir knew it was time to move.

We're so prone to rush things, aren't we? In our culture of instant gratification it's hard for us to "be still, and know that He is God."[5] But if God says no—or even slow down—it's for your own good.

If the request is wrong, God says, "No."

If the timing is wrong, God says, "Slow."

If *you* are wrong, God says, "Grow."

But if the request is right, the timing is right, and you are right, God says, "Go!"

4. act on GOD's will

> But he said to them, "Do not detain me, now that the LORD
> has granted success to my journey. Send me on my way so
> I may go to my master." (v. 56, NIV)

Obedience to revealed truth guarantees guidance in matters
unrevealed. The wind of God is always blowing…but you must
hoist your sail! In the book of Acts, when God spoke to the
apostle Philip with orders to go to the desert, he went—even
though it made no logical sense at the time.[6] We must do the
same. God won't necessarily give you a detailed blueprint. He
will reveal to you as much as you need to know, nothing more,
nothing less.

God leads us step by step, from event to event. It will only be
afterwards, when we look back with the luxury of hindsight, that
we will discover how God led us more than we ever realized or
dreamed. God used important moments of our lives, even times
of crisis, or situations we may have balked at or complained about
at the time, to lead us in His will through life.

5. GOD confirms his will

How did Isaac deal with being a forty-year-old single guy? Here's
a little snapshot from the Bible.

> He went out to the field one evening to meditate, and as
> he looked up, he saw camels approaching. Rebekah also
> looked up and saw Isaac. She got down from her camel and
> asked the servant, "Who is that man in the field coming to
> meet us?"

> "He is my master," the servant answered. So she took her
> veil and covered herself.

> Then the servant told Isaac all he had done. Isaac brought
> her into the tent of his mother Sarah, and he married
> Rebekah. So she became his wife, and he loved her; and
> Isaac was comforted after his mother's death. (vv. 63-67)

So many singles I have known work themselves up into a mad rush-rush to find that right person. And there's certainly nothing wrong with wondering and praying about such a deep, God-given desire. In Genesis 2:18, God said of Adam, literally, "Not good is the aloneness of man." It was God Himself who brought Eve to Adam's side. And if He sees that aloneness is ultimately "not good" for you, He will bring your mate to you, in His perfect timing. But there's nothing wrong with bringing your desire before Him in prayer. You can start praying for that future husband or wife right now.

While you're still single, however, you need to take advantage of your mobility and availability. Paul had these things in mind when he penned these words to the single men and women in the church at Corinth:

> In everything you do, I want you to be free from the concerns of this life. An unmarried man can spend his time doing the Lord's work and thinking how to please him. But a married man can't do that so well. He has to think about his earthly responsibilities and how to please his wife. His interests are divided. In the same way, a woman who is no longer married or has never been married can be more devoted to the Lord in body and in spirit, while the married woman must be concerned about her earthly responsibilities and how to please her husband.
>
> I am saying this for your benefit, not to place restrictions on you. I want you to do whatever will help you serve the Lord best, with as few distractions as possible.
> (1 Corinthians 7:32-35)

Sometimes we think of singles as second class citizens. ("What? You're not married *yet*?") But many of the great movers and shakers of scripture were unmarried. Elijah had no wife, and he shook a nation. The apostle Paul turned his world upside down. Jesus never had a wife. And the list goes on.

The bottom line? While you're single serve the Lord with all your heart. But at the same time, don't feel guilt over your desire for companionship. Wait on the Lord. Jesus said, "Your heavenly Father already knows all your needs, and he will give you all you need from day to day if you live for him and make the Kingdom of God your primary concern" (Matthew 6:32-33, NLT).

Isaac wasn't running around like a chicken with its head cut off, he was meditating in the field. And then…in the very place of meditation and prayer, the beautiful Rebekah appeared on the horizon.

Seeing him, Rebekah said, "Who is this man walking in the field to me us?" Or as it says in the Greg Translation, "Who is that *fox* out there in the field?"
Eliezer replied, "That's my master."

Rebekah wrapped a veil around her face. Could it have concealed a big smile? *Yes, Lord!*

God's plans for you are always better than your plans for yourself. God provided Abraham's son with a beautiful bride, who also had a beautiful heart. And Isaac loved her.

It's a charming love story, but it's much more than that. It's also a picture of God's love for us and His call upon our lives. He will reveal His general will to us in the Bible, He will give us wisdom on specific matters as we wait on Him, and once we feel we have the sense of His direction, He will confirm that in our lives in multiple ways.

He may cause a verse from Scripture to leap out at you from the page, speaking exactly to your situation. He may move obstacles and shift circumstances in such a way that you can recognize His hand clearing the way for you. He may speak to you through a trusted Christian friend, family member, or pastor. God's creativity is endless, and He knows how to move you into the main current of His will if you're ready to wade out into the water with a humble, obedient heart. This story is a beautiful picture of God's love for you, and how He sought you and brought you to Himself.

chosen and treasured

Rebekah was thought of before she even knew it.

Abraham had told his servant:

> "But you shall go to my country and to my family,
> and take a wife for my son Isaac." (v. 24)

In the same way, God thought of us and chose us, the Bride of Christ before we were ever aware of it. Paul reminds us of this in his letter to the church of Ephesus.

> For he chose us in him before the creation of the world
> to be holy and blameless in his sight. (Ephesians 1:4, NIV)

Jesus said "You have not chosen Me, but I have chosen you…." Before you were even aware of His presence, He was thinking of you, loving you, getting ready in His timing to reveal His unique and wonderful plan for your life.

proclaiming the message

Abraham didn't just sit back and wait for Rebekah to come to his son, he sent his servant to seek her out. The one objective of the servant was to announce Abraham's purpose, which was to find a bride for his son.

It's the same with the Lord. He has not only chosen us, but He also sought us out. Make no mistake about it, the Bible clearly teaches predestination. *And it also teaches the free will of man.* It teaches that God has chosen me, but it also teaches that I must choose Him.

> "Choose for yourselves this day whom you will serve…."
> (Joshua 24:15)

> "I have set before you life and death, blessing and cursing;
> therefore choose life, that both you and your descendants
> may live." (Deuteronomy 30:19)

> "Whoever believes in Him should not perish…" (John 3:16)

How then do I reconcile those two contradictory ideas?

I don't.

You don't have to reconcile friends. I just concentrate on what He has told me to do, and leave the "choosing part" up to Him. He has told me to know Him and make Him known, to believe and then to proclaim. He has asked me to simply trust Him and obey Him—not try to unravel the mysteries of the universe. What a relief!

The Bible says: "We are therefore Christ's ambassadors, as though God were making his appeal through us. We implore you on Christ's behalf: Be reconciled to God. God made him who had no sin to be sin for us, so that in him we might become the righteousness of God" (2 Corinthians 5:20, 21, NIV).

Notice the words here: God makes His appeal through us. Christ implores non-believers through us. In other words, the Almighty God of the universe pleads with fallen man through you and me. If this doesn't inspire us, I don't know what will.

the power of the message

There was power in the message Eliezir brought. As a servant, his objective was to simply declare the facts. He was not to add to them or take away from them, just proclaim what was true.

The same is true of each of us. We are to proclaim the Gospel. Paul wrote: "For Christ didn't send me to baptize, but to preach the Good News —and not with clever speeches and high-sounding ideas, for fear that the cross of Christ would lose its power" (1 Corinthians 1:17, NLT).

He is reminding us that there is a distinct power in the simple message of the life, words, death, and resurrection of Jesus Christ from the dead. We often underestimate the raw power the Gospel message has in reaching even the most hardened heart.

Don't underestimate its appeal.

Don't be ashamed of its simplicity.

Don't add to it or take away from it.

Just proclaim it and stand back and watch what God will do.

I have been amazed time and time again how God so powerfully uses this simple yet incredibly profound message to radically change lives. From outright Satanists to moral, yet lost people. From broken families and people addicted to drugs to those deceived by the cults. From the hardened atheist to the deceived cultist. The words of the Gospel, driven home to hearts by the Holy Spirit, is the most powerful message in all the world.

the down payment

Upon accepting the offer of marriage, Rebekah received the down payment of things to come.

> Then the servant brought out jewelry of silver, jewelry of gold, and clothing, and gave them to Rebekah. He also gave precious things to her brother and to her mother. (Genesis 24:53)

In the same way, God sent His Holy Spirit into our lives as a down payment of things to come.

> And you also were included in Christ when you heard the word of truth, the gospel of your salvation. Having believed, you were marked in him with a seal, the promised Holy Spirit, who is a deposit guaranteeing our inheritance until the redemption of those who are God's possession— to the praise of his glory. (Ephesians 1:13-14, NIV)

We have received a down payment on heaven—and it is the most amazing deposit that could ever be made. The Holy Spirit, God Himself, the Third Person of the Trinity takes up residence in our own inner being.

But what does that part about "marked in him with a seal" mean? Back in the first century, when goods were shipped from place to another they would be stamped with a wax seal, imprinted with a signet ring bearing a unique mark of ownership.

It was the same with important documents. If a king sent an important letter to one of his officials, it would be sealed with wax, and imprinted with the royal seal.

If anybody messed with that seal, they would be messing with the king himself. And that was big, big trouble. No one would dare break that seal unless they were the person it was addressed to. In the same way, God has put His royal seal of ownership on us. He has made the down payment, and we will follow through with our full inheritance in Christ.

making the break

Rebekah had to make a break with all that would slow her down or hinder her progress.

Then they had supper, and the servant and the men with him stayed there overnight. But early the next morning, [Eliezer] said, "Send me back to my master."

"But we want Rebekah to stay at least ten days," her brother and mother said. "Then she can go."

But he said, "Don't hinder my return. The LORD has made my mission successful, and I want to report back to my master."

"Well," they said, "we'll call Rebekah and ask her what she thinks." So they called Rebekah. "Are you willing to go with this man?" they asked her.

And she replied, "Yes, I will go."
(vv. 54-58, NLT)

When the work of the Holy Spirit has begun in our lives, Satan tries to stop us. Even close friends and family can be a real snare. Jesus said "If anyone comes to Me and does not hate his father and mother, wife and children, brothers and sisters, yes, and his own life also, he cannot be My disciple" (Luke 14:26-27).

In response to a man who wanted to wait until mother and father died before he followed the Lord, Jesus said, "Let the dead bury their own dead, but you go and preach the kingdom of God" (Luke 9:60).

Rebekah's family took her aside and said, "Will you go with this man?" (Translation: *Are you SURE, honey?*)

And she said, "I will go."

If you deal with one excuse to keep you from completely following Christ, another will invariably take its place. And though God will do what is necessary to bring an awareness of our need for Him, He will not force the issue. He will convict us, speak to us, and most importantly love us, but the ultimate decision lies with us.

Eliezir used no high pressure appeals. He presented the simple facts of the case. But Rebekah said, "I will go!"

She had made up her mind to leave everything she had ever known behind, and travel to a far country to meet a stranger. And the first step of that journey was probably the hardest of all.

But it was probably all forgotten when she looked up one evening and saw her bridegroom walking toward her through the field.

She was home.

chapter five

encounter at peniel: wrestling with GOD

We've all had those moments in life when we look up to heaven with a perplexed or heavy heart and say, "Why?"

Have you ever prayed and prayed for something and no answer came? Maybe it was for a wayward prodigal or an unsaved mate. Perhaps you've asked God again and again for His healing touch on a nagging health problem, or for an understanding of His will in your life. It could be you've been asking God for years to find you a mate, open a door of ministry, or rescue you from a difficult personal circumstance.

In other words, you've desired with all your heart for God to do what *you* want Him to do. And there's not a single thing wrong with that. The Lord wants us to bring our requests to Him. Scripture reminds us that, "You do not have because you do not ask."[7] Clearly, Jesus told us to "keep on asking, and you will be given what you ask for. Keep on looking, and you will find. Keep on knocking, and the door will be opened."[8]

From where you stand, it seems you've been asking for good and worthy things...but for whatever reason, God hasn't budged. *And sometimes it feels like you're wrestling with Him.*

It could be that you've felt God's leading to do a certain thing or pursue a specific direction, and you've refused. You really don't want to grant Him full access to that particular area of your life, and you've actually found yourself fighting and resisting Him. Once again, you feel like you're in a wrestling match with Someone bigger and stronger than you.

Is wrestling with God a bad thing, then?

Not necessarily.

a turning point

Years ago, it happened with a man named Jacob. His wrestling match with the Almighty began with resisting and ended with resting. At first, he tried to move God his way, but in the end Jacob moved God's way. Clinging to the Lord, he said, "I will not let You go until You bless me" (Genesis 32:26).

The book of Hosea gives this brief account of that wrestling match: "Before Jacob was born, he struggled with his brother; when he became a man, he even fought with God. Yes, he wrestled with the angel and won. He wept and pleaded for a blessing from him. There at Bethel he met God face to face, and God spoke to him" (Hosea 12:3-4, NLT).

Maybe that's where you find yourself today. Fighting with God. Trying to run from Him or turn away from His work in your life. Deep in your heart, you know the Lord is pointing you in a certain direction, but you're dragging your feet. You don't want to go. You want your will, not His.

Here's what you need to know about that situation.

It won't work.

You can't win it.

Any wrestling match you have with the Lord will end in failure. *Your arms are too short to box with God.* But don't let that discourage you. The fact is, God's plan for you is infinitely better than your plan for yourself.

Perhaps you find yourself trying to do what you want to do in life, and you keep facing crisis after crisis. One step forward and three steps back. Maybe something fairly traumatic has happened in your life recently that has really gotten your attention. God has given you a wake up call beyond anything you've experienced for a long time.

If you had a little perspective on where you are right now, if you could somehow get above time and space and look down on your life, you might conclude that you're approaching a watershed moment, a turning point, an epiphany. The Bible might call it a revelation.

Let's think together in the pages of this chapter what
He may be seeking to say to you.

jacob's back trail

Isaac and Rebekah's fraternal twin boys, Jacob and Esau,
were as different as they could be—not "identical" in any
sense of the word.

Jacob, the second born, was given his name at birth when he
emerged from the womb clutching his brother's heel. His parents
must have believed this to be something significant, because the
name Jacob means "Heel-catcher." The name might also be rendered Contender, Supplanter, or Grabber. A strange name for
a baby boy, you might say. Yet it truly became prophetic of his life.

At first glance, you might conclude that Jacob's brother Esau
was the more admirable of the two. Hairy as a bear, he was a
man's man who loved hunting and the open fields. And Jacob?
Well, he liked to hang around the family tent and help Mom in
the kitchen.

But as we all know, first appearances can so often be decep-
tive. Time would show that Jacob—in spite of serious flaws—was
a righteous man, and Esau—in spite of his apparent qualities—
was an ungodly man.

Things aren't always as they initially appear. It isn't difficult
to think of men and women who began the Christian life with
such great promise, only to later crash and burn at the end.

Esau may have looked like he had it all together, but Scripture
says he was a profane and godless man who in the end lost all
that really mattered. Jacob's life was no walk in the park, either.
Not many people have had more starts and stops than he had
through his long life. But in the end, this son of Isaac finished
well, literally limping across the finish line in the race of life.

From before his birth, God had clearly promised the
birthright to Jacob[9]. Yet instead of waiting on God's provision

and timing, Jacob took matters into his own hands, catching his brother at a vulnerable moment and persuading him to sell the birthright—for a bowl of stew!

> Make sure that no one is immoral or godless like Esau. He traded his birthright as the oldest son for a single meal. And afterward, when he wanted his father's blessing, he was rejected. It was too late for repentance, even though he wept bitter tears. (Hebrews 12:16-17, NLT)

Then to add insult to injury, Jacob conspired with Rebekah to steal the blessing of the blessing of Isaac intended for his Esau.

Jacob's basic issue was that he kept resisting doing God's work in God's way. He was always conniving, plotting, and scheming, and the repercussions of those actions would haunt him for the rest of his life. As a result of what Jacob did to his brother, Esau was ready to kill him. Realizing this, Rebekah dispatched her second-born to visit her brother Laban in faraway Paddan-aram.

And Jacob would never see his mother again.

stairway to heaven

> On his way to the land of the north, Jacob had an unusual encounter with God. As he slept one night out in the open country, God gave him a stunning vision he would never forget.

Meanwhile, Jacob left Beersheba and traveled toward Haran. At sundown he arrived at a good place to set up camp and stopped there for the night. Jacob found a stone for a pillow and lay down to sleep. As he slept, he dreamed of a stairway that reached from earth to heaven. And he saw the angels of God going up and down on it.

At the top of the stairway stood the LORD, and he said, "I am the LORD, the God of your grandfather Abraham and the God of your father, Isaac. The ground you are lying on belongs to you. I will give it to you and your descendants. Your descendants will be as numerous as the dust of the earth! They will cover the land from east to west and from north to south. All the families of the earth will be blessed through you and your descendants. What's more, I will be with you, and I will protect you wherever you go. I will someday bring you safely back to this land. I will be with you constantly until I have finished giving you everything I have promised." (Genesis 28:10-15, NLT)

God was essentially saying to his wayward servant, "Jacob, please, I can do it Myself. Believe it or not, I can do this work without even you!"

So often, we get the idea that God needs us. As a result, we will try to step into the role of the Holy Spirit, and "help Him out" a little.

Listen, God doesn't need your help. He doesn't need my help. He doesn't need *anyone's* help—He's the Almighty! In the Psalms He says of Himself:

> I know all the birds of the mountains,
> And the wild beasts of the field *are* Mine.
> If I were hungry, I would not tell you;
> For the world is Mine, and all its fullness.
> (Psalm 50:11-12)

Jacob seemed deeply moved by the vision. He knew this was no ordinary dream, and the experience awed him.

> Then Jacob woke up and said, "Surely the LORD is in this place, and I wasn't even aware of it." He was afraid and said, "What an awesome place this is! It is none other than the house of God —the gateway to heaven!" The next morning he got up very early. He took the stone he had used as a pillow and set it upright as a memorial pillar. Then he poured olive oil over it. He named the place Bethel—"house of God." (Genesis 28:16-19, NLT)

You would think such a dramatic encounter with God would have changed Jacob forever, wouldn't you? Think of it! A vision of heaven, with awesome heavenly beings strolling up and down a stairway to the stars—and God Himself standing at the top of the stairs! That ought to make an impression on anyone. We can easily imagine a shaken Jacob saying, "All right, Lord. I'm a changed man. No more deception, no more trickery, no more trying to help You out."

Initially, that night at Bethel did seem to have a profound effect on him. Afterwards, a literal translation of Scripture says that "he lifted up his feet." His heart was full of joy, and he moved into a new chapter of his life with fresh confidence.

But even an experience with God doesn't guarantee we won't fall back into our old ways or our old habits. So it was with Jacob. All too soon, he slipped back into his old identity as Heel-Grabber.

reaping what we've sown

Finally arriving at his destination, Jacob saw the beautiful Rachel and sent the other men off to water the sheep to assure he would be alone with her. Deciding he wanted to marry her (not one for waiting), he went to her father Laban.

In Laban, Jacob finally met his match—and got a strong dose of his own medicine. The con-artist met the master con-artist (they deserved each other). Laban demanded seven years labor for Rachel, *which seemed as but a few days for the love he had.*

On the wedding night, however, Laban pulled a classic bait-and-switch. Jacob thought he was honeymooning with his beloved Rachel, but Laban had secretly substituted Leah, the older sister. It was the custom (he explained later) that the firstborn was entitled to be married first.

What was that about the rights of the firstborn?

Jacob had to learn a principle he himself had violated, and the lesson didn't go down very easy. The deceiver had been deceived, and had to work for the woman he loved for another seven years.

After being with Laban twenty years, Jacob demanded his wages that he might return home. Through a complicated sting operation, Jacob managed to coral many more sheep than the miserly Laban had planned to give him.

Jacob wanted to go home, and God gave him the green light.

Then the LORD said to Jacob, "Return to the land of
your fathers and to your family, and I will be with you."
(Genesis 31:3)

How could the message have been any more straightforward?
Return...and I will be with you." It was a crystal clear word from
God. Wouldn't you imagine that with an iron-clad promise like
that, Jacob could have said his goodbyes with a smile and set
off for Canaan at an easy pace?

Of course, that is *not* what happened. Instead of leaving
well with handshakes all around, Jacob and his family "got
out of Dodge" while Laban and sons were shearing sheep in
a distant field. Instead of counting on God's blessing and protection, Jacob pretty much slipped away like a fugitive from justice.

Why the secrecy? Because he was afraid. "If I let Laban know
I'm about to leave, he'll strip me of everything I own" (again,
not trusting God). What Jacob did not know, however, was that
his beloved Rachel had stolen the household gods. It's not clear
if Rachel did this as an act of spite because of her anger over the
way Laban had treated her husband, Jacob, or if she still believed
in the idols herself. Maybe she felt in taking them she was essentially covering all her bases.

Laban found out, however, and didn't spare the horses chasing
Jacob's tribe down on the road to Canaan. Once again, Jacob found
himself reaping the hard consequences of his conniving ways.

How many lessons does it take? How many times did he have
to be broken? (It's a question we might ask ourselves, isn't it?)
You would think he would be saying, "Okay Lord—I get it!
Let me up from the mat, You've pinned me!"

out of the frying pan...

Jacob was able to work out his differences with his father-in-law,
but there was still some more reaping to do. It was time to deal
face-to-face with his brother he had betrayed, Esau. Jacob could
not retreat. He couldn't run. He had nowhere to go but forward.

And forward was where his brother Esau was. The brother he had cheated out of his birthright and blessing some twenty years earlier.

In a sense, he'd been running from Esau for twenty years, hiding out in Haran. This just reminds us that we will reap what we sow.

Scripture is clear on this subject. It might be a verse we wish would go away sometimes, but it will be there forever, so we might as well face up to it.

> Don't be misled; remember that you can't ignore God and get away with it: a man will always reap just the kind of crop he sows! If he sows to please his own wrong desires, he will be planting seeds of evil and he will surely reap a harvest of spiritual decay and death; but if he plants the good things of the Spirit, he will reap the everlasting life that the Holy Spirit gives him. (Galatians 6:7-9, TLB)

If you sow a crop of righteousness and integrity you will reap that. If you sow a crop of deceitfulness, manipulation, and self-effort, you will reap that, too. Jacob had done more of the latter, and there was no escaping it. But he had received a word from God who told him it was time to return.

It was time for Jacob to own up to his past—to come face to face with the wrongs he had done. And Jacob was about to find out the hard way the truth of Proverbs 18:19: "A brother offended is harder to win than a strong city, and contentions are like the bars of a castle."

That's not to say we shouldn't try, for that's what the Lord would have us do. The Bible tells us, "If it is possible, as much as depends on you, live peaceably with all men."[10]

As he approached the dreaded moment of meeting Esau, Jacob was about to encounter the Lord in a way beyond anything he'd ever experienced. It was time for a turning point in his life. This show that God will meet us at whatever level He finds us in order to lift us to where He wants us to be.

Do you need God to come to you right now? What problem are you facing? He will be more than sufficient.

A friend of mine recently had his father die. Then a few days later, his son died in a tragic accident. One Monday he buried his father, the next Monday, his son. What could be harder than this to face? I offered what words of comfort I could find, but frankly, I didn't really know exactly what to say. He wrote me a note in response, and spoke of how Jesus had been enough. Then he added *"more than enough!"*

That's what Jesus said to Paul regarding the troubling thorn in his flesh. *"My grace is sufficient for you."* God will give you what you need when you need it. He will come to you in just the right way, as He did for Jacob. The Bible says, "Let us therefore come boldly to the throne of grace, that we may obtain mercy and find grace to help in time of need" (Hebrews 4:16).

To Abraham, the pilgrim, God came as a traveler. You remember the three mysterious visitors that came to Abraham's tent before the destruction of Sodom and Gomorrah. The Lord was one of them.[11] To Joshua, the general, Jesus came as the commander of the Lord's army, with sword drawn.[12] And to Jacob? Well, here was a man who had, figuratively speaking, wrestling with people most of his life…his father, his brother, his father-in-law, and even his two wives. So how did the Lord appear to Jacob?

As a wrestler.

It was as if He was saying to Jacob, you want to wrestle? Do you want some of this? I'll show you wrestling!

In the psalms, David spoke of how the Lord reveals Himself in different ways to different people.

> With the merciful You will show Yourself merciful;
> With a blameless man You will show Yourself blameless;
> With the pure You will show Yourself pure;
> And with the devious You will show Yourself shrewd.
> (Psalm 18:25-26)

the all-night wrestling match

And he arose that night and took his two wives, his two female servants, and his eleven sons, and crossed over the ford of Jabbok. He took them, sent them over the brook, and sent over what he had. Then Jacob was left alone; and a Man wrestled with him until the breaking of day. Now when He saw that He did not prevail against him, He touched the socket of his hip; and the socket of Jacob's hip was out of joint as He wrestled with him. And He said, "Let Me go, for the day breaks."

But he said, "I will not let You go unless You bless me!"

So He said to him, "What is your name?"

He said, "Jacob."

And He said, "Your name shall no longer be called Jacob, but Israel; for you have struggled with God and with men, and have prevailed."

Then Jacob asked, saying, "Tell me Your name, I pray."

And He said, "Why is it that you ask about My name?" And He blessed him there.

So Jacob called the name of the place Peniel: "For I have seen God face to face, and my life is preserved." (Genesis 32:22-30)

With whom did Jacob wrestle that night? It was no mere angel! This was a preincarnate appearance of God's Son. Jacob was wrestling with Jesus Christ! He called the place Peniel, which means "I have seen God face to face."

When Jacob finally got alone with God, things began to happen.

Bible commentator C. H. Macintosh wrote, "To be let alone with God is the only true way of arriving at a just knowledge of ourselves and our ways. No matter what we may think about ourselves, or what others may think of us, the great question is what does God think of us?"

When we get away from all the distractions, alone with God, we can get a correct assessment of ourselves. Some are afraid to do this! So they clutter their lives with activities. Remember Martha? She could have been sitting at the feet of Jesus, like her sister Mary, but instead she distracted herself banging around pots and pans in the kitchen.

Have you been alone with God lately? In our "connected society" do we even have a moment to think? We are barraged with information on demand, e-mail, instant messaging, cell phones, Blackberries, and on and on. The use of Blackberries is so rampant they have been described as "crack-berries"! We are all communicating with each other—constantly! People walk around with little devices clipped on their ears. You see them walking down the street by themselves, talking loudly and gesturing with their arms. They look like they're talking to you…or to themselves.

It's crazy. Are all these conversations necessary? Are we afraid to be alone with our thoughts? Or, more to the point, are we afraid to be alone with God? Where can God get a word in edgewise?

So here is the conniving plotting, scheming, Jacob all alone with God. The Lord shows up, and Jacob starts wrestling with Him! This would be like a three year old going up against Hulk Hogan. If you score a point or two, it's only because he *let you*. I suspect that God would gain a little advantage, and then allow Jacob to feel that he was gaining.

This went on and on all night long. But it was necessary. Jacob needed to reach the point where he had no more strength. The Lord continued on and on until Jacob was just about spent. Then God touched him, knocking his hip out of joint.

It was a life-changing moment for the old heel-grabber. In that instant, a change took place. Now, instead of fighting with God, Jacob clung to Him! He had a death-grip on the Lord, and would not let go.

With the night almost over, and dawn on the eastern horizon, the Lord said, "Let Me go, the day is breaking." Jacob responded, "I will not let You go unless You bless me!"

In surrender to God's plan, Jacob would find what he'd always wanted.

This is the proper kind of wrestling with God—where you are desperately calling out to Him and not giving up because you believe what you ask for is His very will. Paul mentioned it when he saw this level of get-after-it prayer in one of his co-workers in ministry. "Epaphras...is always wrestling in prayer for you" (Colossians 4:12, NIV).

Again Paul alludes to this kind of persistence and struggle in prayer in Romans 15: "Dear brothers and sisters, I urge you in the name of our Lord Jesus Christ to join me in my struggle by praying to God for me. Do this because of your love for me, given to you by the Holy Spirit" (v. 30, NLT).

Yes, prayer can sometimes be a struggle. In that light, we start to see wrestling matches all over scripture.

We see Abraham, praying with persistent intensity for Sodom.[13]

We find Moses spending forty days and nights fasting and pleading mercy for Israel.[14]

We find Elijah, pressed to the ground with his face between his knees, praying seven times for God to send rain.[15]

We see this persistent intensity of prayer again and again with David, when he calls out, "Hear my prayer, O LORD, and give ear to my cry; do not be silent at my tears."[16]

So don't give up! Keep praying for that work of God in your life, where you will be more like Jesus. Keep praying for that healing for you or someone else, unless God directs otherwise. Keep praying for the salvation of that loved one. Keep praying for that spiritual awakening our country needs to experience.

After Jacob had lost this match, the Lord asked him an unusual question. *"What is your name?"* (Genesis 32:7).

Why did the Lord ask this of Jacob? Had he suddenly been afflicted with short term memory loss so that he couldn't remember his own name?

No, it wasn't that. God asked because for Jacob to state it was an *admission*—and one he didn't really want to make. As we have said, the name Jacob meant "heel-catcher, supplanter, grabber." In essence, the Lord was asking Jacob, "Are you going to continue living up to your name, continually deceiving others? Or will you admit what you are and let Me change you?"

This was a question only Jacob could answer. And it's a question God asks each of us as well.

"do you want to be made whole?"

The apostle John tells the story of a man who had suffered from a severe disability for thirty-eight very long years. For much of that time, he had waited by a little pool of water in Jerusalem called Bethesda. The local story about that place said that an angel would periodically appear and stir up the water—and whoever scrambled into the water first would be healed.

So the disabled man sat there day after day, night after night, just waiting and hoping.

Then Jesus walked by.

The Lord saw him lying there, and knew he already had been in that condition a long time. He said to him, "Do you want to be made whole?"

Why would Jesus ask such a question. Wasn't it obvious a man in this state would want to change?

Not necessarily.

As strange as it may seem, there are many people today who don't want help. They like the lifestyle they've chosen. They find a certain comfort there. They feel security in the darkness. It's home to them just like a pigsty is home to a pig. It's comfortable, and they really don't want to come to the light or make changes in their lives. This pattern continues on until eventually these people become so hardened in their sin that they prefer the dark ways of eternal death.

Scripture says, "A man who remains stiff-necked after many rebukes will suddenly be destroyed—without remedy" (Proverbs 29:1, NIV). Along that same theme, Oswald Chambers wrote: "Sin enough and you will soon be unconscious of sin."

That was the case with Jacob. When God asked him, "What is your name?", He was essentially saying, "Do you want to be a Heel-Grabber forever? Do you really want to live this way—conniving, scheming, lying, manipulating—or would you like to let Me take control and change your life?"

God will not force His will or His way in our lives. He asks us, "Are you finally willing to give *Me* control? Jesus said, "Take My yoke upon you and learn of me…." A yoke is a steering device. Jesus was saying, "Let Me steer and guide your life! Are you willing?"

I can't help wondering what Jacob must have thought when that all-night wrestling match began. Was it a bandit? Was it one of Laban's angry sons? Was it an assassin sent by Esau—or maybe Esau himself? The more he wrestled however, the more he came to understand that this was no ordinary mugger in the dark. Something big was in the works!

Jacob wasn't wrestling with God to get something from Him, rather God was wrestling with Jacob to get something. What was it? *Surrender.* It was to reduce Jacob to a sense of his nothing-ness, to cause him to see what a poor, helpless, and weak person he really was.

Before Jacob ever walked the planet, God brought a man named Job to the same place. After his own long wrestling match with the Almighty, he surrendered with the words: "I am nothing—how could I ever find the answers? I will put my hand over my mouth in silence. I have said too much already. I have nothing more to say" (Job 40:4-5, NLT).

Perhaps the main reason God challenged Job to a wrestling match was for you and me. In Jacob, we learn the all important lesson that our true strength lies in admitting our weakness.

Why? For the same reason He sent most of Gideon's army home, or told the great Namaan to strip off all his clothes and dunk seven times in the muddy Jordan. Or repeatedly went out of His way to find obscure instruments to work through like Jeremiah, David, or Peter. Because, as He says in 2 Corinthians 12:9, "My grace is sufficient for you, for My strength is made perfect in weakness." A more literal reading of the verse tells us: *My grace is enough for you, for power is moment by moment coming to its full energy and complete operation in the sphere of weakness.*

Again, by losing you win.

Through defeat you find victory.

Have you ever had God wrestle with you when you wanted your way or were persisting in some course that you knew displeased Him? Maybe that's even happening to you right now. I'll give you a hint of what the outcome will be. You're going to lose, and lose big!

But don't let that frighten you. Again, God's plan and purpose for your life is far better than any you may have thought up for yourself.

Jacob had finally surrendered. Instead of fighting with the Lord he asked for His blessing. God had brought him from cunning to clinging, from resisting to resting. Jacob had now been brought to the end of his resources, and having surrendered, he was given a new name...*Israel.*

Scholars differ on the meaning of the name. It has been variously translated as "One who God commands," "Let God rule," "One who fights victoriously with God," or "A prince with God." Still another renders it, "God's fighter."

Whatever the precise meaning of Israel, it's clear that a complete surrender took place in Jacob's relationship with God. God was saying "You are no longer the heel-catcher, the supplanter. Now you are a Prince with God, God's fighter!"

And now in the long-dreaded encounter with Esau—and beyond—God Himself would be his advocate. And from that time on, the countless descendants of Jacob would be known by his new name, Israel.

Jacob may have lost the wrestling match, but by doing so, he scored the biggest victory of his life. At last, Jacob had surrendered himself. He won by losing and now was able to go on in new strength as he walked in God's power, will, and timing.

This is precisely what Jesus meant when He said, "He who finds his life will lose it, and he who loses his life for My sake will find it."[17]

In his second letter to the church at Corinth, Paul spoke about a wonderful-if-mysterious aspect of the Christian life. He wrote:

> And we, who with unveiled faces all reflect the Lord's glory, are being transformed into his likeness with ever-increasing glory, which comes from the Lord, who is the Spirit. (2 Corinthians 3:18, NIV)

At a lonely place called Peniel, Jacob saw God's face, and his life changed forever. Paul is saying that we too are changed when we gaze into His face. The face of God always changes Jacobs to Israels, grabbers to receivers, supplanters to princes and princesses.

No doubt about it, we all have our Esaus. We all have those situations in life that cause us great fear and stress. But when we have spent time alone with God, seeing His face, it can transform and prepare us for whatever lies ahead.

Surrender to God and discover His plan for your life. If you've felt like you can't win for losing, try losing to the God who loves you and experience the biggest win of your life.

chapter six

encounter in egypt: standing strong in life's storms

We all know the story of Cinderella.

A poor, unloved girl grows up in a house with her cruel stepmother and jealous step-sisters. Through a set of stunning circumstances, she is given the opportunity to attend the royal ball at the palace. But what will she wear? Her clothing is little more than rags.

Depending on which version you've heard, she is aided by a bunch of mice and three fat little fairies—blue, green, and pink—who pitch in to create a stunning evening gown. Cinderella goes to the ball looking like a princess, meets the handsome prince, loses her glass slipper, becomes the object of a kingdom-wide woman hunt, and ends up in the forest with seven dwarves.

Or…something like that.

Now that's called a fairy tale, and you might tell yourself that it's beyond belief and really just for fun. It's an enjoyable bedtime story and makes a great Disney cartoon, but that's about as far as it goes.

But I know a story that's far more extraordinary than any Cinderella tale—whatever the version. And what makes this story all the more remarkable is that it's true.

This is a story that has the earmarks of a great novel—a page turner. The author weaves all of the elements of an enthralling plot through its pages: jealousy, betrayal, sex, intrigue, an international crisis—and dreams come true! Throw attempted murder, a seductress, and accusations of rape into the mix, and you've got a real summer sizzler.

But it's so much more than that. It's also an historical account of real people working through situations that remind us of trials in our own lives. And if those things weren't enough, it's a story that reveals the Lord at work in the daily experience of His own. The hand of God shows up in every scene, ruling and overruling the decisions people make. And in the end, God builds a hero, saves a family, and creates a nation that will bring blessing to the whole world.

Cinderella is pablum, truly kids' stuff, compared to the real-life drama springing out of the first book in the Bible. The story of Joseph is the classic rags to riches tale, as he rose from complete obscurity and unbelievable adversity to the second most powerful position in all of Egypt—the superpower of his day. Here was a young man who clung to his faith in the living God, even in the face of gross injustice and crushing disappointments. As a result, God's blessings on his life were mighty.

the rise of a hero

Joseph's life initially showed little promise. A simple shepherd boy, twelfth of thirteen children—he was a young man apparently given to visions of grandeur. As any other teenager, Joseph enjoyed sleeping. But there was a difference. When Joseph experienced a couple of strange dreams, he firmly believed they were from God Himself.

And they were.

To his older brothers, it appeared this kid had his "head in the clouds," always trying to dodge a hard day's work. Yet young Joseph was on his way to becoming God's man. Daring to be a dreamer, he was transformed from a favored (perhaps pampered), immature, naïve teenager into a great world leader.

If anyone could have ever had an excuse for turning out bad, it was Joseph. He grew up in the midst of a family dominated by lying, deceit, immorality, manipulation, and even murder. He could have turned out rotten to the core—and blamed his stepmom, dad, brothers, and like many others, even God Himself.

For seventeen years he put up with these challenges, and surprisingly turned out to be a godly young man with a sterling character. Joseph's life is a strong illustration of Psalm 76:10:

Human opposition only enhances your glory,
for you use it as a sword of judgment. (NLT)

Do you live in an ungodly, messed up, dysfunctional home
that might qualify for an appearance on the Jerry Springer show?
Take heart. It can't be any worse than Joseph's home! God preserved and blessed him, and He can do the same for you.

As I look back on my own upbringing, being raised in a home
of seven divorces and alcoholism, I can see how God preserved
me. Even when I was a little boy, He was working in my life,
setting me into an earnest "search-mode," as I sought to understand the meaning of life.

As with Joseph, the age of seventeen was a turning point in
my life. For that was the age I was when I gave my life to Jesus
Christ after hearing the Gospel on my high school campus.

Looking back now, I really don't blame anyone for anything.
In fact, God has been able to use my past as I've pursued my
ministry. I can better understand the skepticism that so many
have toward the Gospel, for I once had it myself.

sold down the river

> Now Jacob dwelt in the land where his father was a
> stranger, in the land of Canaan. This is the history of Jacob.
> Joseph, being seventeen years old, was feeding the flock
> with his brothers….Now Israel loved Joseph more than all
> his children, because he was the son of his old age. Also he
> made him a tunic of many colors. (Genesis 37:1,2,3)

You would have thought that Jacob's own painful personal
experience with favoritism in his growing up years would have
convinced him to never repeat that destructive pattern. What
a mess that had been! Isaac had openly favored Esau, Jacob's
twin brother, while mother Rebekah clearly loved Jacob the
most. And it ended up tearing the family apart.

It could happen to any of us. If we're not careful, if we're not drawing our wisdom and strength from the Lord, we can fall back into the same old negative parenting techniques that we hated so much growing up. Jacob favored Joseph because he was the son of the only woman he ever really loved—his beautiful, long-departed Rachel. He doted on the boy, indulging him and spoiling him to the point that his older eleven brothers were thoroughly disgusted.

Adding salt to that wound, Jacob presented Joseph with a multi-colored tunic—or "coat of many colors," as it says in the King James Version. Yet another translation calls it "a richly ornamented robe."

This was more than a case of young Joseph getting the nicest school clothes in the family. Basically, this was a long-sleeved garment that extended to the angles. Obviously you can't do to much manual labor in a fancy coat like that. In Joseph's day, the working garb was a short, sleeveless tunic, leaving the arms and legs free. When Joseph wore that fancy coat around, it would be like going to work in a tuxedo. In fact, we read in another place in scripture that this kind of garment was worn by royalty.

It was a clear statement that Jacob planned on giving "firstborn" status to Joseph, the youngest. By giving a coat of this sort to Joseph, Jacob was essentially saying, "You don't have to work like your brothers."

No wonder his siblings became bitter! No doubt their resentment grew deeper with every passing day. But matters went from bad to worse when Joseph took upon himself the role of family informant. That *really* enraged them.

> Joseph…was feeding the flock with his brothers. And the lad was with the sons of Bilhah and the sons of Zilpah, his father's wives; and Joseph brought a bad report of them to his father. (v. 2)

As a young Christian, I could be very hard on people. Several people took me aside in those days, pointing out how I was always correcting others. Do I do that today? I hope not! I'm banking on the assumption that as you grow in knowledge, you also grow in grace as well. It's not a matter of lowering your standards, it's more an issue of finding balance. Paul tells us to "let your conversation be gracious and effective so that you will have the right answer for everyone" (Colossians 4:6, NLT).

In the eyes of Joseph's brothers, however, he was nothing less than a snitch. But the fact of the matter is, Joseph was a godly man. Scripture says "Everyone who does evil hates the light, and will not come into the light for fear that his deeds will be exposed."[18] If you have taken an unpopular stand for righteousness as a Christian, you already know what it's like to be ostracized, rejected, mocked, or even hated.

However honest and godly Joseph may have been, you would think he might have used a little more tact! Showing up in his fancy Dad-loves-me-best coat to check on the brothers he had already reported on probably wasn't the best idea. The story of Joseph's betrayal might have been different if he had left the cloak hanging up in a closet at home on that trip.

These brothers were so filled with anger and venom they couldn't say a kind word to him. Was he oblivious to this? And what about reporting the dreams that had his brothers bowing down to him, paying him homage? Couldn't he have kept those things to himself? Was he actually flaunting his favored position in the family, standing there in his multi-colored tunic, speaking of ruling over everyone—a mere seventeen-year-old boy?

Then to make matters worse he related yet another dream, this time to his dad. In this second dream, Joseph saw all his brothers and even his father and stepmother bowing before him. In reality, that was a prophetic dream from the Lord, because that is exactly what happened years later, when he became the vice-Pharaoh.

But sometimes it's not wise to talk freely about the all the dreams, visions, or things that God has revealed to you. Some-times the wiser course is to be like Mary, the mother of Jesus, when she was confronted with the supernatural. Scripture says she "quietly treasured these things in her heart and thought about them often."[19]

When Joseph finally found his brothers in that remote place, their thoughts immediately turned to murder.

> Then his brothers went to feed their father's flock in Shechem. And Israel said to Joseph, "Are not your brothers feeding the flock in Shechem? Come, I will send you to them."
>
> So he said to him, "Here I am."
>
> Then he said to him, "Please go and see if it is well with your brothers and well with the flocks, and bring back word to me." So he sent him out of the Valley of Hebron, and he went to Shechem.
>
> …So Joseph went after his brothers and found them in Dothan. (Genesis 37:12-17)

The brothers went off to tend to the sheep in Shechem. Genesis 34 tells us that this was a place of dark memories. It was the very area where their sister Diana had been raped— and where Simeon and Levi committed mass murder in retaliation. As you might imagine, there was still "bad blood" between the sons of Jacob and the dwellers in that area. Jacob, probably concerned about their safety, sent Joseph to check up on them and bring word back.

Big mistake.

> Now when they saw him afar off, even before he came near them, they conspired against him to kill him. Then they said to one another, "Look, this dreamer is coming! Come therefore, let us now kill him and cast him into some pit; and we shall say, 'Some wild beast has devoured him.' We shall see what will become of his dreams!"
> (vv. 12-14, 17-20)

"Here comes the dreamer!" they mocked. They had almost decided to kill him, but instead threw him into a pit. Providentially, a caravan of slave traders were passing by, and so they sold their brother for 20 pieces of silver. Taking Joseph's beautiful coat, the brothers soaked it in goat blood, and sent it to Jacob, saying a wild animal had killed him.

Jacob was devastated. He went into deep mourning and would not be comforted. It crushed him to the very core.

And Joseph? He found himself on his way to Egypt, in chains. He had been abandoned by man—even by his own brothers. *But not by God.* In fact, God would begin to show Himself strong on Joseph's behalf through the many trials that were to come. One day, the young man would come to learn the truth about God expressed by Corrie Ten Boom: "There is no pit so deep that He is not deeper still."

stranger in a strange land

Now Joseph had been taken down to Egypt. And Potiphar, an officer of Pharaoh, captain of the guard, an Egyptian, bought him from the Ishmaelites who had taken him down there. The LORD was with Joseph, and he was a successful man; and he was in the house of his master the Egyptian. And his master saw that the LORD was with him and that the LORD made all he did to prosper in his hand. So Joseph found favor in his sight, and served him. Then he made him overseer of his house, and all that he had he put under his authority. So it was, from the time that he had made him overseer of his house and all that he had, that the LORD blessed the Egyptian's house for Joseph's sake; and the blessing of the LORD was on all that he had in the house and in the field. Thus he left all that he had in Joseph's hand, and he did not know what he had except for the bread which he ate. (Genesis 39:1-6)

Sold into slavery by his own brothers, Joseph soon found himself in a county and culture he didn't know, surrounded by a language he didn't understand. He had truly gone from feasting to famine. His world came crashing down overnight! Think about it. One night Joseph was safe and secure, tucked in his own bed, the next night possibly shackled and shivering as he was carted off like an animal to be sold on the open slave market. The bottom had dropped out for Joseph in a mere matter of hours. But that wasn't the end of the story. Not by a long shot. He was soon to experience success beyond anything he had ever known.

His dreams were going to come true.

Egypt was a completely pagan country filled with religious superstition. The people recognized at least 2,000 gods and goddesses, including the Pharaoh himself. The Egyptians were great builders, and the rulers conscripted both slaves and their own citizens for vast building projects. Into this teeming city of wickedness and idolatry came Joseph, a wide-eyed country boy far from home.

As providence would have it, Joseph was purchased by a man named Potiphar, a captain of the guard and high-ranking Egyptian official. He most likely served as head of the military police assigned as the royal bodyguard—the secret service of his day.

Clearly, Potiphar was not a man to be trifled with. Yet Scripture tells us, "The LORD was with Joseph, and he was a successful man; and he was in the house of his master the Egyptian" (Genesis 39:2).

Do you remember reading about the blessed man in Psalm 1?

He shall be like a tree
Planted by the rivers of water,
That brings forth its fruit in its season,
Whose leaf also shall not wither;
And whatever he does shall prosper.
(v. 3)

That was Joseph. Whatever he did, prospered. Success followed him like his shadow. He had the "Midas touch" because he kept his priorities straight. Though he had been stripped of his coat, he had not been stripped of his character. And he clearly did *not* hide his faith from his powerful, intimidating master.

Scripture gives us these incredible words:

> And his master saw that the LORD was with him and
> that the LORD made all he did to prosper in his hand.
> (Genesis 39:3)

Potiphar, a hardened, pagan military officer, recognized and acknowledged the hand of the living God on this teenager's life. The Lord was with him. Joseph was really a model of how a Christian should function in the workplace. Faithful and hard-working, he was a young man who did his very best.

Augustine wrote: "Preach the Gospel, and when necessary use words." Because of his hard work and integrity, Joseph was promoted and given a great platform for his faith. Perhaps Solomon had Joseph in mind when he wrote: "Do you see a man who excels in his work? He will stand before kings; he will not stand before unknown men."[20]

Joseph's behavior and performance were so outstanding and above reproach he became Potiphar's executive assistant! But all of this hard work was not only a blessing to the household, but to Joseph as well. Had he stayed home with his pampering father, Joseph might not have developed the kind of character that comes from hard work and obeying orders. This was a time of testing in his life, for if he was going to learn to be a leader, he must first learn how to be a servant.

Maybe you find yourself in such a time right now—laboring somewhere in obscurity, keeping long hours and doing hard work without much recognition. You wonder at times, *Will my day ever come? Does anyone even notice what I'm doing here? Will God ever use me?* Know this…Your Father, who sees you in secret, will one day reward you openly.

Needless to say, Satan wasn't one bit happy about this turn of events in Joseph's life. Perhaps sensing God's significant plans for this young man, Satan had set out to utterly destroy Joseph—first by casting him in a pit, then by selling him as a slave. But everything Satan threw at Joseph seemed to boomerang, and work out for good. Now the son of Jacob found himself in good standing in the household of a powerful Egyptian official.

But the Evil One wasn't through yet. He was about to strike another devastating blow.

when temptation comes

We never really know when we're about to be hit with a serious test. You can wake up on an ordinary morning, have your usual bowl of cereal, take your every-day route to school or the office, and begin your walk through what would seem to be a day like a hundred other days before it.

Yet by the afternoon, you could find yourself in the biggest crisis of your life. That's the way it must have been with Joseph, as he went about his normal duties as an overseer in Potiphar's household.

What he was about to face was in many ways a more difficult trial than being sold into slavery by his own brothers. As a robust, healthy, twenty-something young man, with hormones running at their peak, he was about to be blindsided by sexual temptation. How would he handle it? How would he handle this new position of prestige and power?

When we are struggling to get ahead in life or find ourselves facing some kind of crisis, we often turn to God in complete dependence and weakness. We realize just how frail, vulnerable, and susceptible we really are, and we cling to Him. But when success comes, when the health is good, when the bills are paid and the skies are blue, we sometimes tend to forget the very God who brought us to that point.

Greater success leads to greater times of vulnerability. Prosperity, acclaim, and success can put us directly in the cross-hairs of hell. All of us should walk very, very carefully in life, but men and women who have reached new levels of success and prominence in the business world or in ministry need to be especially alert.

Our human tendency is to begin to take such things for granted, to let down our guard a little, to ease back. Before long, we get lazy, sloppy, slothful. And that is when the enemy springs a surprise attack, firing his flaming arrows at our faith, commitment, and integrity.

Think for a moment about the life of David. When did temptation hit him between the eyes? It wasn't when he was a lonely shepherd boy, watching over the flock out in the wilderness (and wrestling the occasional lion or bear). It wasn't when he was running for his life from the paranoid King Saul, hiding in desolate canyons and gloomy limestone caves. No, David got hit when he was at the *top* of his game. He was king. He was rich. He was famous. He was powerful. He was well loved. He had a powerful ministry leading his nation to the throne of God in praise and worship.

But one fateful spring day, after sending Joab out to lead the army (instead of leading it himself), David decided to kick back and take it easy for awhile. Feeling a little restless that evening, he took a walk on his rooftop terrace….

As it turned out, David was a much safer man dealing with adversity than with prosperity. And so it is for many of us. Our enemy knows very well that "pride goes before destruction, and a haughty spirit before a fall."[21]

the proposition

And it came to pass after these things that his master's wife cast longing eyes on Joseph, and she said, "Lie with me."

But he refused and said to his master's wife, "Look, my master does not know what is with me in the house, and he has committed all that he has to my hand. There is no one greater in this house than I, nor has he kept back anything from me but you, because you are his wife. How then can I do this great wickedness, and sin against God?"

So it was, as she spoke to Joseph day by day, that he did not heed her, to lie with her or to be with her.

But it happened about this time, when Joseph went into the house to do his work, and none of the men of the house was inside, that she caught him by his garment, saying, "Lie with me." But he left his garment in her hand, and fled and ran outside. And so it was, when she saw that he had left his garment in her hand and fled outside, that she called to the men of her house and spoke to them, saying, "See, he has brought in to us a Hebrew to mock us. He came in to me to lie with me, and I cried out with a loud voice. And it happened, when he heard that I lifted my voice and cried out, that he left his garment with me, and fled and went outside." (Genesis 39:7-15).

Joseph was certainly a good looking young guy. Verse 6 says that "Joseph was handsome in form and appearance." Another translation says, "Joseph was a very handsome and well-built young man."[22]

Joseph may have been both shocked and flattered by this offer from Pot's wife. Those advances had to be a tremendous ego boost. Imagine how a slave would feel being approached by a beautiful, powerful woman. No doubt, Mrs. Potiphar wife was attractive and alluring.

Keep in mind that for about ten years now, he's been saturated with Egyptian values. Those old values he had learned from his parents must have seemed a little rusty or archaic by this time. At the very least, they would have seemed quite distant. Besides that, *no one would ever know.* They were completely alone. He could have easily rationalized, "When in Egypt, *walk like an Egyptian.*"

But deep in Joseph's heart was the conviction that even if no one else might find out about their little fling, *God* would know.

"How then can I do this great wickedness, and sin against God?"

Joseph knew very well that God was watching. And God was and is watching each and every one of us as well.

Verse 8 tells us that "he refused." Now that may seem impossible to do to in a moment of intense temptation…but it isn't. Joseph had evidently made that determination a long time before the lustful Mrs. Potiphar cornered him in the bedroom. Joseph recognized that temptation is not a sin; it's a call to battle.

What made this particular temptation so difficult was that it went on and on. The Bible says, "She kept putting pressure on him day after day, but he refused to sleep with her, and he kept out of her way as much as possible" (Genesis 39:10, NLT).

Maybe after he had resisted that first time, he breathed a sigh of relief. But the woman was relentless. And you can bet she knew how to dress and how to present herself in a way that would make it as difficult as possible on the young man.

But if she propositioned Joseph again and again, he resisted again and again. Temptation—any temptation—can be effectively resisted! As scripture says "Submit yourselves, then, to God. Resist the Devil, and he will flee from you."[23]

The reason it seems like we "can't resist" at times is because we have set ourselves up for a fall. We have filled our minds with lustful things, and we're like rags doused in gas waiting for the match. For temptation to properly work its evil there must be a desire on our part. The apostle James writes: "But each one is tempted when he is drawn away by his own desires and enticed. Then, when desire has conceived, it gives birth to sin; and sin, when it is full-grown, brings forth death" (James 1:14-15).

For Satan to succeed, we must listen, yield, and most importantly *desire* what he offers. Satan will use different types of bait to tempt us, but remember, it's not the bait that constitutes sin, it's the bite! Potiphar's wife dropped the bait day after day in front of Joseph, but he kept saying "no." How? I see four points in Joseph's successful battle with temptation.

1. everyone will be tempted

We may think that if we're really spiritual or mature in the Lord, we won't be tempted any more. But the very opposite is true. If you are truly spiritual you *will* be tempted. Why? Because you are a direct threat to Satan and his agenda.

At the very beginning of His ministry, Jesus was led into the wilderness to be tempted by the Devil. At the end of His ministry, on the cross, Satan tempted Him through the thief and the soldiers who challenged Him to come down from the cross if He was really the Son of God.

If Jesus faced temptation from the beginning to the end, so will we. An old minister was asked by a young man, "Preacher, when will I cease to be tempted by sins of the flesh?"

The wise old man said, "Son, I wouldn't trust myself until I'd been dead three days!"

2. sin has consequences

"Look," he told her, "my master trusts me with everything in his entire household. No one here has more authority than I do! He has held back nothing from me except you, because you are his wife."(Genesis 39:8-9, NLT)

Joseph was loyal to the man who had trusted him and been so good to him. He thought about how this sin would affect others. When he could have easily thought only of himself ("I want this…I deserve this"), Joseph rather said, "I can't do this, because it would hurt Potiphar."

In the same way, when you're tempted to have that affair, or have sex before marriage, it might be a good idea for you to stop and think about somebody besides yourself. Your spouse, your family, your parents, the other person, their family. *Everyone* is affected by unfaithfulness and sexual immorality.

And how about thinking about that person's spouse, or spouse to be? And what about their children?

Listen, you have no right take something that belongs to them. And most importantly, think of the damage this can do to the cause of Christ. What a terrible witness it is when a believer falls in this way. In fact, it's just the same as giving ammunition to our enemies. As the prophet Nathan told David, "You have given the enemies of the LORD great opportunity to despise and blaspheme him."[24]

And just for the record, if you begin a relationship with an act of betrayal and immorality—no matter who this person may be—it will not work out. One researcher has stated that of those who break up their marriage to marry someone else, 80 percent are sorry later. Of those who do marry their lover—which happens only about 10 percent of the time—nearly 70 percent will end up divorcing their new spouse. Of that 25 to 30 percent who stay married, only half of them are happy.[25]

Committing adultery throws open the door to a storm of pain and tragedy, with the effects rolling on for the rest of your life, and the lives of your children as well.

3. GOD's standards are absolute

The years, decades, and centuries may come and go, but God's standards don't change. It didn't matter that Joseph had been mistreated and had a rough childhood. It didn't matter that he was far from home. It didn't matter that he was lonely. It didn't matter that the Egyptian culture was completely immoral. And it didn't matter that Joseph's life was completely taken from him and that he was forced to be a slave.

Wrong is wrong.

Given enough time and enough motivation, every one of us is capable of rationalizing almost anything. If we want something bad enough, if we entertain the desire long enough, we can talk ourselves into lies that would have shocked and repelled us at an earlier point in our lives.

I'm lonely. I need this.
He/she has a selfish, unresponsive spouse.
God wants me to be happy.
I can always ask for forgiveness later.

If he had been so inclined, Joseph could have come up with a list of justifications for adultery as long as your arm. But he refused to indulge such thoughts, and denied them room to take root in his soul.

4. all sin is against GOD

"How then can I do this great wickedness,
and sin against God?"

This—not fear of the consequences—should be our strongest deterrent against sin. Yes, dreading what God might do or allow to happen to us if we turn against Him is certainly a factor. *But the greatest deterrent against sin is a consuming love for God.* Our response to temptation is an accurate barometer of that love.

The psalmist wrote: "Let those who love the LORD hate evil, for he guards the lives of his faithful ones."[26]

Our Father hates sin, and so should we as His children. The Bible tells us to "Abhor what is evil. Cling to what is good" (Romans 12:9). We may try to justify certain sins—jealousy, anger, revenge, and so on—against "certain people," because we feel they deserve it. But as David said, "Against you, and you alone, have I sinned; I have done what is evil in your sight."[27]

Besides that, Potiphar was not a believer, and Joseph knew that. And to violate God's will in this matter would irreparably damage his witness. Though God will forgive us, others may not—at least not so quickly—and a tarnished reputation is very difficult to repair.

Joseph could have played around the edges with adultery, dabbling in it, like Samson who thought he could "always handle it." He, like Lot, was "worn down by sin" and was soon so hooked he failed to notice how Delilah was no longer even subtle. *"Please tell me what makes you so strong and what it would take to tie you up securely."*[28] Delilah must have been one enticing lady to keep Samson coming around the way he did.

Joseph wasn't afflicted with brash self-confidence, either—like Simon Peter. *"Even if all fall away on account of you, I never will…. Even if I have to die with you, I will never disown you."* (Then what was he doing just a few hours later by that charcoal fire?) Scripture says, "Let him who thinks he stands take heed lest he fall."[29] Joseph, however, knew very well that he was vulnerable—so he fled!

There's an old Chinese proverb that says: "He who would not enter the room of sin must not sit at the door of temptation." This is basically a no- brainer. It would be like walking across a field and coming upon a coiled rattlesnake, looking at you through those glazed, beady eyes, ready to strike. What do you do? Try to negotiate with the rattler? Reach some sort of a compromise perhaps? Do you just stand there, or maybe even approach it to show how strong you are? If so, I hope your will is in order! No, if you have half a brain you back off and run as fast as you can.

Flee temptation—and don't leave a forwarding address. Every temptation is an opportunity to flee to God.

> And so it was, when she saw that he had left his garment in her hand and fled outside, that she called to the men of her house…. (v. 13)

Joseph preferred to leave his jacket behind rather than lose his hide. And this young man's "No" to her was a "Yes" to God.

Are you being tempted right now in some area of your life? Does it seem like too much to handle, too strong to resist? That's not true! God promises us that He will *not* give you more than you can handle (see 1 Corinthians 10:13).

As we, like Joseph, resist each temptation, we will grow stronger with every passing day. Not in our own strength but in God's. Recognizing our vulnerability, we will distance ourselves from anyone or anything that could potentially pull us down.

You'll be glad you did in the long run. It's far better to shun the bait than to struggle on the hook.

the lesson of joseph's brothers

What happened to Joseph's brothers, back in Egypt?
As you zero in on the end of the story in Genesis 42-50, it's
obvious that they were never able to put their treacherous act
behind them. Through the long years, the knowledge of what
they had done gnawed away at their souls like acid. I'm guessing
they could never look their dad straight in the eye from that day
forward. Whenever Joseph's name came up, it must have been
like a knife twisting in their hearts. Even on the best days of
harvest or feasting or gatherings of the family, there would
always be that shadow of guilt and regret.

We sold our own brother as a slave.
We've deceived our father for years.
He's surely dead now, and it's our fault.

I think there are at least two lessons to be learned
in the latter chapters of Joseph's story.

1. never let envy and jealousy get a foothold in your life.

These are among the more subtle but deadly sins in the satanic
arsenal. They're like time bombs ticking away, waiting to explode.
Left unchecked, these sins can lead to far worse. The apostle
James wrote: "For wherever there is jealousy and selfish ambition,
there you will find disorder and every kind of evil."[30]

As we saw in Chapter Two, envy is what filled Cain's heart
resulting ultimately in murder. Envy is what drove the Pharisees
to crucify Jesus. Pilate accurately diagnosed the situation:
"He knew for envy they had delivered Him" (Matthew 27:18)

What a wicked thing jealousy is. Shakespeare called it
"The green eyed monster that mocked." William Penn said,
"The jealous are troublesome to others; a torment to themselves."

The sad truth is, our old nature doesn't like to see others
succeed sometimes. Paul warned some of the people in Corinth:
"You are still controlled by your own sinful desires. You
are jealous of one another and quarrel with each other.

Doesn't that prove you are controlled by your own desires? You are acting like people who don't belong to the Lord."[31]

An ancient Greek story tells of a statue erected in honor of a famous athlete. A rival athlete was so enflamed with envy he vowed to destroy the monument. So every night in the dark, he chiseled at its base to weaken its foundation. But when it finally fell, it fell on him, crushing him.

So nip envy in the bud before it crushes you! F. B. Meyer has the best advice: "At the first consciousness of sin, seek instant cleansing in the precious blood of Christ...."

2. GOD will work all things together for good.

"Do not be afraid, for am I in the place of God? But as for you, you meant evil against me; but God meant it for good, in order to bring it about as it is this day, to save many people alive." (Genesis 50:19-20)

It's easy for us to see (now) how God worked all the events of Joseph's life for good, because most of us know the end of the story. But *he* didn't! All he knew was that he was a boy who had been sheltered by his doting father from many of the harsh realities of life, and now he had lost it all—probably forever. He was a common slave in a faraway country, and all his dreams had turned to ashes.

In every way, however, Joseph's life illustrates the truth of Romans 8:28:

And we know that all things work together for good to those who love God, to those who are the called according to His purpose.

"We know...."

Those things that happen to us in life have nothing to do with fate, random chance, or dumb luck. Doris Day's old hit song expresses the attitude of many: *"Que sera, sera, whatever will be, will be. The future's not ours to see. Que sera, sera...."*

While it's true that we can't see over the horizon and know the future, we can know that there is a master plan for every believer, custom-designed by the Creator Himself. *I may not know what the future holds, but I know who holds the future.*

God works "all things" in life for our good—not just the "good things" or happy things. The psalmist wrote: "for all things serve you."[32]

This doesn't mean that all things are good things, for there are many circumstances and occurrences in our lives that, in themselves, aren't good at all! They are painful and bitter. Yet ultimately their place in the whole pattern of God's divine purpose will cause them to be resolved ultimately into good—on our behalf.

The phrase "work together" in Romans 8:28 could better be translated "are working together." In other words, there are no breaks or lapses in God's good plan for your life. It's not as though it's operational today, but goes off-line tomorrow. God is always paying careful attention to even the smallest detail of your life, and is in complete control of all circumstances that surround you.

Our God never sleeps. As it says in the psalms, "Behold, He who keeps Israel shall neither slumber nor sleep" (Psalm 121:4).

Aren't you glad God doesn't take a sabbatical and put you on voice mail when you pray? You know…push #1 if you need forgiveness…push #2 if you need healing…push #3 if you need direction…push #4 if you have another problem.

Our God is always on duty. David could readily say, "God is our refuge and strength, a very present help in time of trouble."

Corrie Ten Boom used to show the reverse side of an embroidered bookmark which seemed to be nothing but a senseless mass of tangled threads. Then she would turn the bookmark over, where the threads spelled out in a beautiful design, "God is love."

That was Joseph's experience. Tangled years. Impossible knots. A jumble of seemingly meaningless and random trials. But at the end of it all…the Master Craftsman revealed the beauty, worth, purpose, and healing of His design.

And so it will be with you, as you place your whole life—past, present, and future—into His skillful hands.

chapter seven

encounter at pharaoh's court: rejecting a compromised life

there is no soft, politically correct way to say it: Prior to coming to know Jesus Christ, you were under the power and control of the Devil. He had been jerking your chain for quite a long time…

…promising pleasure, he brought you misery…

…promising fun, he brought you guilt…

…promising life, he brought you death….

And the most clever strategy of all was causing you to think he didn't even exist! You thought *you* were in control all this time.

Then one day it hit you like a lightning bolt from heaven, and your eyes were opened. You not only realized there was a Devil, but more importantly, a God he was trying to keep you from. A God who loved you enough to send His own Son to die on the cross.

You realized you could find meaning and purpose in this life, and the absolute hope of heaven in the next. You carefully thought about it. You counted the cost. And finally, you took the plunge and made a stand for Jesus.

I hope you weren't expecting a standing ovation in hell.

the evil empire strikes back

The Devil is not happy with your decision to follow Christ. In fact, it enrages him. He's lost one of his own! But he's not going to take it lying down. He will hit back—hard. Someone has said, "Conversion has made our hearts a battlefield." The genuine believer may be known by his inward warfare as well as his inward peace. In fact, if you are *not* experiencing this spiritual tug of war, that in itself is cause for concern.

What we are facing here is a spiritual battle with a very real adversary. So if you are feeling beat up, if you've been experiencing what seems like more than your share of temptations and attacks, cheer up! It's a strong indicator that you are doing the right thing and heading in the right direction.

Satan knows all too well he cannot overpower God. His strategy, then—really from the beginning of time—has been to draw men and women out from under God's protection and covering. If he can persuade you to live in the realm of your will, your plans, your perspective, and your own strength, then he has you where he wants you…and you are in grave danger.

Know this: the Devil may be evil, but he is no fool. He's not about to tip his hand and show you what he's really up to in your life. He didn't want you to believe in Jesus in the first place, but once you give your heart to Christ, he has to concede that battle. But that doesn't mean the war is over. Now his purpose in your life is to persuade you to compromise, and in the process, spiritually neutralize you.

So he will try to take you one bite at a time, through the subtle yet extremely effective medium of compromise. This technique is well illustrated in the story before us in this chapter.

one-on-one with pharaoh

This is the story of Moses and his confrontation with the Pharaoh over the deliverance of the Israelites from Egypt.

The Lord had told Moses to go back to Pharaoh's court, back to the very place where he had grown up, for a face-to-face encounter with the king who may have been the most powerful man in the world at that time.

God had made it very clear to Moses that he was to take the Jews a good three days journey from the land of the bondage. And He warned him that this battle of wills with Pharaoh wasn't going to be a walk in the park.

"You must go straight to the king of Egypt and tell him, 'The LORD, the God of the Hebrews, has met with us.

Let us go on a three-day journey into the wilderness to offer sacrifices to the LORD our God.'

"But I know that the king of Egypt will not let you go except under heavy pressure. So I will reach out and strike at the heart of Egypt with all kinds of miracles. Then at last he will let you go. (Exodus 3:18-20, NLT)

The Lord was warning Moses that Pharaoh would harden his heart, *and would not let them go.*

In this we have a picture of the Devil and his unwillingness to let his captives go. Let's consider the passage together.

Afterward Moses and Aaron went in and told Pharaoh, "Thus says the LORD God of Israel: 'Let My people go, that they may hold a feast to Me in the wilderness.'"

And Pharaoh said, "Who is the LORD, that I should obey His voice to let Israel go? I do not know the LORD, nor will I let Israel go."

So they said, "The God of the Hebrews has met with us. Please, let us go three days' journey into the desert and sacrifice to the LORD our God, lest He fall upon us with pestilence or with the sword." (Exodus 5:1-3)

So…the big moment had finally come.

Moses may have thought he could just stroll into Pharaoh's court, demand the release of God's people, and that would be that. Pharaoh would comply, and the Israelites would be on their way to the land of milk and honey.

But not so fast.

Pharaoh wasn't about to let go easily. And Moses was about to run into a brick wall. It's often the same for us. Sometimes we think the will of God should always be smooth sailing. After all, if Almighty *God* is involved in this thing, then He'll just steamroll all the obstacles out of the path.

But sometimes He doesn't…for His own good reasons.

Not only did Pharaoh flatly refuse to release the Jews, he actually increased their workload!

Ever have one of those bad days when nothing seems to be going your way? Or have you ever been certain that something is the will of God, but instead of the doors opening as you expect, they seem to slam shut in rapid succession?

That's surely how Moses must have felt that day. There he was, doing the hard thing, obeying God and boldly walking into the inner sanctum of this world superpower, and demanding the release of the Israelites. Now Moses knew this wasn't going to be a one-two-three game of hopscotch. But he certainly hadn't anticipated a complete disaster! And that's what he got.

By the end of Exodus 4, Moses and his brother Aaron had already met with the leaders of Israel, and told them of their God-given mission. Moses even did miracles to show he had indeed been sent by God. The miracles had the desired effect, and they agreed together and prayed. Moses and Aaron went before Pharaoh with the blessing of the people and the leading of God.

> So Moses and Aaron went in to Pharaoh, and they did so, just as the LORD commanded. And Aaron cast down his rod before Pharaoh and before his servants, and it became a serpent.
>
> But Pharaoh also called the wise men and the sorcerers; so the magicians of Egypt, they also did in like manner with their enchantments. For every man threw down his rod, and they became serpents. But Aaron's rod swallowed up their rods. And Pharaoh's heart grew hard, and he did not heed them, as the LORD had said. (Exodus 7:10-13)

In verse 3, the Lord says, "I will harden Pharaoh's heart." What does that mean? Does it mean Pharaoh really had no choice in the matter—that he was little more than a robot, and just did what God made him do? The word "harden" could also be translated, *strengthen*, or *stiffen*. So what was God really doing? He was strengthening Pharaoh in the decision the Egyptian king had *already made*.

a heart of cement

As we will see, Pharaoh began to harden his heart when Moses and Aaron performed this first of many miraculous signs. He hardened his heart further when the magicians counterfeited the signs. He even hardened it when his magicians could not counterfeit the signs. It just got harder and harder—like quick-dry cement.

The Lord had given him more than enough evidence to convince him that the "gods of Egypt" were false, and the God of Israel was the true and living God. God was giving Pharaoh a chance to cooperate. He was dealing in love and longsuffering with Pharaoh. Scripture records the true heart of God:

> As surely as I live, says the Sovereign LORD, I take no pleasure in the death of wicked people. I only want them to turn from their wicked ways so they can live. Turn! Turn from your wickedness, O people of Israel! Why should you die? (Ezekiel 33:11-12, NLT)

God was leaving the door open for Pharaoh to change his mind, *but he would have none of it*. To turn from the truth is to become more thoroughly entrenched in darkness. Pharaoh saw miracles and heard the Word of God, and that brings responsibility. He had to *do* something with what he had seen and heard. He had to consider the evidence right before his eyes and make a decision. But one rejection led to another and another. And with every rejection, his heart turned further away from the Lord…until he came to that point where the door was shut and locked, and he had no inclination to change—ever.

The writer of the Hebrews issues this warning: "You must warn each other every day, as long as it is called 'today,' so that none of you will be deceived by sin and hardened against God" (Hebrews 3:13, NLT).

We often think the worst thing that can happen to a person is if they become entangled in some sinful lifestyle with drugs, illicit sex, alcohol, partying, and so on. But appearances can be deceiving. If that individual still retains a soft heart and a tender conscience, there is hope that he or she may hit bottom, and in desperation reach out to God. But once a person becomes hard—deliberately steeling their heart and turning away from the truth—the hope of reaching them with the Good News grows fainter and fainter.

And how do we become hardened? *By continued exposure to the truth of God and a refusal to obey and respond to it.*

In other words…you know it's true, yet you don't accept it. You accept it intellectually, yet you don't respond. You become hardened by the very truth that should have softened you. As with Pharaoh, you become judged by the very message that should set you free.

God had sent a series of ten plagues or judgments to bring Pharaoh to his senses, each one gaining in intensity as Pharaoh allowed his heart to cure like concrete in the afternoon sun. What makes this drama even more interesting is that there was a specific strategy behind these judgments. Each was leveled at a specific "god" of Egypt.

The nation of Egypt claimed millions of gods, worshiped in thousands of temples across the land. God leveled these judgments to show the emptiness and futility of any god when compared with the true and living One.

The account tells us that Moses' rod became a serpent. The serpent was one of the special creatures in Egyptian religion—particularly the cobra, which was a symbol of immortality.

But note how Satan countered this miracle.

But Pharaoh also called the wise men and the sorcerers; so the magicians of Egypt, they also did in like manner with their enchantments. For every man threw down his rod, and they became serpents. (Exodus 7:11-12)

Here is something we need to understand about Satan: He is an *imitator.*

knock-offs from hell

Our adversary will try to stop a work of God altogether, but if that doesn't work, he will *imitate* it. In this way, he not only deceives people, he minimizes the power and glory of God. The purpose is to neutralize the impact of our life and testimony— and to divert us from the truth.

Do you desire a relationship with God? You need to be careful…and discerning. Satan offers a plethora of false religions laden with rituals and symbols—with just enough truth to keep you from *real* truth.

Jesus told a story about a farmer who had an enemy. Late one night after the farmer had sown his fields with wheat, the enemy slipped in under the cover of darkness and sowed tares— or darnel seeds—throughout the same fields. As the tares begin to sprout, they look just like wheat—you can't tell the difference. But in the end, the tares actually uproot the wheat, and destroy the crop.

That's one of Satan's strategies. He has flooded the market with cheap substitutes of truth, each with enough accuracy to make it appealing, but enough poison to make it deadly. Cyanide with a dark chocolate coating.

One of the sobering things this passage in the book of Exodus teaches is that Satan can do miracles, too, imitating the signs and wonders Moses and Aaron had performed in the presence of Pharaoh. These miracles were completely within his power.

This is why I am always suspicious of so-called "miracle ministries." Satan is in the miracle business, too! None of the apostles had "miracle ministries"…they had a simple call to proclaim Jesus. The signs would follow their ministries, but they were never the primary focus. You never read in the book of Acts where the apostles would announce a "healing service" ahead of time. Rather, God healed where and when He chose to—often as a direct confirmation of the message of the Word of God.

Scripture tells us that in the last days, the Antichrist will have a "miracle ministry."

> This evil man will come to do the work of Satan with counterfeit power and signs and miracles. He will use every kind of wicked deception to fool those who are on their way to destruction because they refuse to believe the truth that would save them. So God will send great deception upon them, and they will believe all these lies. (2 Thessalonians 2:9-11)

The second satanic beast in the book of Revelation was also given power to perform "great and miraculous signs, even causing fire to come down from heaven to earth in full view of men" and "because of the signs he was given power to do…he deceived the inhabitants of the earth" (Revelation 13:13, 14, NIV).

In view of these powerful counterfeits, the apostle John warns us, "Do not believe every spirit, but test the spirits , whether they are of God; because many false prophets have gone out into the world" (1 John 4:1). God's Word is our measuring stick.

Let's look now at the various plagues God sent to Egypt.

the ten plagues

plague 1: the nile river turns to blood.

God directed Moses to stand on the bank of the Nile and wait for Pharaoh to join him there. Moses was instructed to tell Pharaoh that he had been sent by God to deliver the Israelites. Then he described the impending judgment:

"Thus says the LORD: 'By this you shall know that I am the LORD. Behold, I will strike the waters which are in the river with the rod that is in my hand, and they shall be turned to blood. And the fish that are in the river shall die, the river shall stink, and the Egyptians will loathe to drink the water of the river.'"

Then the LORD spoke to Moses, "Say to Aaron, 'Take your rod and stretch out your hand over the waters of Egypt, over their streams, over their rivers, over their ponds, and over all their pools of water, that they may become blood….'"

But not sooner had the judgment been leveled against Egypt than Pharaoh's court magicians duplicated it.

Then the magicians of Egypt did so with their enchantments; and Pharaoh's heart grew hard, and he did not heed them, as the LORD had said. And Pharaoh turned and went into his house. Neither was his heart moved by this. (Exodus 7:16-19, 22-23)

How did they do it? How did these pagan magicians duplicate the miracle of turning water into blood? Slight of hand? Smoke and mirrors? Demonic power? It would have been a bit more impressive if they had been able to turn the bloody Nile water back into clean water, rather than simply duplicating God's judgment. (Whoever said sin made sense?)

But the enchanters did accomplish one thing. It was all the excuse Pharaoh needed to once again harden his heart to God's word.

The ancient Egyptians revered the Nile River as a god. Not only that, the river was basic to life itself. Well-water in that day was often contaminated, so the Egyptian depended on the Nile for all his water needs—bathing, cooking, cleaning, laundry, and of course drinking.

To strike the Nile was to strike at the very heart of Egypt. And it also showed that their so-called "god" had no power to help them.

plague 2: an invasion of frogs.

God told Moses to go back to Pharaoh and demand the release of the Israelites or all of Egypt would be covered in *wall-to-wall frogs.*

Once again Pharaoh refused to budge. Believe it or not, even the frog was a god to the Egyptians. (For that matter, so was the dung beetle.) The frog deity (no, it wasn't Kermit) was called "He-get." This goddess of the resurrection, fertility, and childbirth had the head of a frog. In this judgment, God was essentially saying, "You want gods? I've got gods for you." And the invasion was on.

> "I will send vast hordes of frogs across your land from one border to the other. The Nile River will swarm with them, and they will come out into your houses, even into your bedrooms and right into your beds! Every home in Egypt will be filled with them. They will fill your ovens and your kneading bowls; you and your people will be immersed in them!" (Exodus 8:2-4, TLB)

Immersed in frogs! Can you imagine?

When I lived in Hawaii as a young boy, we used to have lots of frogs. It was always an adventure having one in the house and stepping on it in your bare feet. But the Egyptians couldn't walk anywhere without stepping on countless, slimy, croaking frogs. They were in their ovens, their dishes, even their beds. You try to sleep at night and you've got frogs crawling across your face.

Pharaoh's magicians, however, copied this miracle, too. They couldn't get rid of the frogs, but they could evidently summon more of them. (Just what everyone needed.)

This time, however, God at least had Pharaoh's attention. He asked Moses to entreat God to *get rid of those frogs,* and then they could discuss releasing all the Jews from captivity. So Moses and Aaron cried out to the Lord, and the frogs all croaked, *en masse.* They gathered the dead frogs together in great heaps and the Bible says *the land stank.*

But when Pharaoh saw that there was relief, he hardened his heart yet again, and refused to heed the word of the Lord.

This is so typical of many non-believers. They will call on God to get them out of some crisis, resulting from their own sinful choices. They will make great and lofty promises of what they will do in return—after God rescues them. Then, when God comes through, they shrug their shoulders, chalk it up to coincidence, and go back to their old ways.

I heard about a hospital chaplain who kept a record of some 2,000 patients with whom he had visited, all apparently in grave condition, who had responded to gospel and showed signs of repentance. But among those who rallied and returned to health, only *two* followed through on their commitment to follow the Lord.

Pharaoh somehow convinced himself that the water-turned-to-blood and the invasion of frogs were some freak anomalies of nature, and his heart went back into lock-down.

And then came the gnats.

plague 3: "gnats all, folks."

Then the Lord said to Moses, "Tell Aaron, 'Stretch out your staff and strike the dust of the ground,' and throughout the land of Egypt the dust will become gnats." They did this, and when Aaron stretched out his hand with the staff and struck the dust of the ground, gnats came upon men and animals. All the dust throughout the land of Egypt became gnats. But when the magicians tried to produce gnats by their secret arts, they could not. And the gnats were on men and animals. (Exodus 8:16-18, niv)

This third plague came with no warning at all. Oftentimes in His grace and mercy God will warn us of what is coming if we continue in sin, giving us time to repent. But if He sees an ongoing, willful pattern of outright disobedience, He just might spring a surprise attack.

These gnats (or lice, in some translations) were apparently biting, stinging insects that penetrated the nostrils and ears of their victims—and every square inch of skin that happened to be exposed. This was especially hard for the Egyptians, who were fanatical about cleanliness. The priests would frequently wash and shave their bodies in order to be acceptable to their gods. And now they were crawling with bugs!

Note also that these plagues were getting progressively worse. The plague on the Nile was a blow to everyone, but people adapted and got by. The frogs were a gross nuisance. People were sickened by them, but no one was hurt.

But these gnats…this was becoming unbearable.

Interestingly, Pharaoh's magicians could not duplicate this plague. They told their boss, "This is the finger of God."[33]

With that strong pronouncement from his own inner circle, would Pharaoh begin to think about repenting? Would he still harden his heart?

In fact, he would. A man or woman's heart can grow so hard to God that only the most radical measures will get their attention.

plague 4: enter…the swarm

And the LORD said to Moses, "Rise early in the morning and stand before Pharaoh as he comes out to the water. Then say to him, 'Thus says the LORD: "Let My people go, that they may serve Me. Or else, if you will not let My people go, behold, I will send swarms of flies on you and your servants, on your people and into your houses. The houses of the Egyptians shall be full of swarms of flies, and also the ground on which they stand…." And the LORD did so. Thick swarms of flies came into the house of Pharaoh, into his servants' houses, and into all the land of Egypt. The land was corrupted because of the swarms of flies. (Exodus 8:20-21, 24)

If you're reading from the New King James Bible, you will note that when Scripture says "swarms of flies," the words *of flies* are in italics, meaning, they weren't in the original.

In other words, the Lord brought *swarms* into the house of Pharaoh and into all the land.

The Hebrew words for swarm means "mixture," speaking of a massive jumble of creepy, crawly, multi-legged, tentacled insects. This would include spiders, fleas, ticks, and flying beetles. (The first instance, perhaps, of "Beatlemania.")

But something very interesting happened with this plague. God intervened in an astounding way for His people. Within the Lord's message to Pharaoh were these pointed words: "And in that day I will set apart the land of Goshen, in which My people dwell, that no swarms of flies shall be there, in order that you may know that I am the LORD in the midst of the land. I will make a difference between My people and your people. Tomorrow this sign shall be" (Exodus 8:22-23).

This swarm of creepy crawlers swept every corner of Egypt except Goshen. Goshen was bug free.

Once again, Pharaoh had to admit he was outgunned— or outplagued. But rather than waving the white flag and surrendering to God, he simply changed his tactics, offering a series of compromises. In this, we see a picture of the Devil's strategy to bring us down…a little here, and a little there.

> Then Pharaoh called for Moses and Aaron, and said, "Go, sacrifice to your God in the land."
>
> And Moses said, "It is not right to do so, for we would be sacrificing the abomination of the Egyptians to the LORD our God. If we sacrifice the abomination of the Egyptians before their eyes, then will they not stone us? We will go three days' journey into the wilderness and sacrifice to the LORD our God as He will command us."
>
> So Pharaoh said, "I will let you go, that you may sacrifice to the LORD your God in the wilderness; only you shall not go very far away. Intercede for me" (Exodus 8:25-28)

What had God specifically commanded Moses and the Israelites? "We will go three day's journey into the wilderness and sacrifice to the LORD our God as He will command us."

But Pharaoh, like the proverbial used car salesman, tried to work the angles.

"Sure, go sacrifice. *But do it in the land.*"

"Fine. Go ahead and follow your God. *But don't go very far.*"

Wasn't he being fair-minded and reasonable? Not at all, because any compromise of obedience to God's commands is *disobedience.*

God had specifically commanded a three-days journey into the wilderness—the whole nation, young and old, along with their livestock and children. God wanted ample room between the people and their Egyptian overlords.

But Pharaoh wanted to play "Let's Make a Deal," and tried to draw Moses in with a few concessions. They could worship their own God if they wanted to. They could go a little ways away. Wasn't that reasonable?

No. It was a trap. You don't make deals with the Devil. If God calls for a complete break, *He means a complete break.*

Do you see how subtle the enemy's tactics can be? If he can't get us to go completely his way, he will seek to draw us just a little bit in his direction. It's not a complete denial of what we know is right and true…it's just a compromise. We push back from our old habits, our old lifestyle, or our old unbelieving crowd, but we don't make a clean break. The Devil says to us, "Fine, believe in God if you must. Do your little religious thing if it makes you feel better. But be practical about it! Don't be a fanatic. You can have your cake and eat it too."

The Bible, however, warns us against such compromises. In the book of Ephesians, Paul says, "Do not give the Devil a foothold."[34]

That's all he's looking for, you know. A foothold. A toehold. A chink in your armor. Give him an inch, and he'll take a mile. Give him a minute, and he'll take an hour…or a day…or a decade. You cannot make deals with Satan. You will always lose if you do.

The Bible says, "You cannot drink from the cup of the Lord and from the cup of demons, too. You cannot eat at the Lord's Table and at the table of demons, too" (1 Corinthians 10:21, NLT).

How we need to guard our hearts on this issue! The apostle Paul reminds us that Satan seeks to outwit us with his schemes.[35] For instance…let's say you're sharing the gospel with someone who is dragging you down spiritually. It might be a romantic relationship (a mistake). At some point, you wisely decide to break it off, only to have the man or woman respond, "But I'm getting closer to coming to Christ! Don't cut me off—pray for me."

In Exodus 8:28, Pharaoh wrapped up his little compromise offer with the words, "Intercede for me." *Pray for me, Moses.*

If Moses hadn't been on his guard, he might have thought, "Well…Pharaoh is softening. He wants me to pray for him. Maybe this little compromise wouldn't be so bad." But that's not what happened. Moses certainly agreed to intercede for the king. He said: "As soon as I leave you, I will pray to the LORD" (8:29, NIV). But he wasn't fooled—and he wasn't willing to walk a single inch away from the Lord's clear commands.

What are we saying here? We should never shy away from trying to influence and win people to Christ. But if we yoke ourselves to them, if we compromise our faith or our convictions to please them, it is *we* who will be pulled down, they won't get pulled up.

Paul stated this clearly in his letter to the believers in Corinth:

Don't team up with those who are unbelievers. How can goodness be a partner with wickedness? How can light live with darkness? What harmony can there be between Christ and the Devil? How can a believer be a partner with an unbeliever? And what union can there be between God's temple and idols? For we are the temple of the living God. As God said:

"I will live in them and walk among them. I will be their God, and they will be my people. Therefore, come out from them and separate yourselves from them," says the Lord. (2 Corinthians 6:14-17, NLT)

If Pharaoh couldn't keep them *in* Egypt, he would at least try to keep them *near* it. Why? So they would still be under Egypt's influence…and because it would be easier to reel them back in again. The fact is, if you're not willing to "go far away," then you'd better not go at all.

plagues 5, 6, and 7: pestilence, boils, and hail

Pestilence on the livestock and boils on everyone was followed by a severe hailstorm. How severe? This storm would have made prime time on the Weather Channel for weeks on end.

> The LORD sent thunder and hail, and lightning flashed down to the ground. So the LORD rained hail on the land of Egypt; hail fell and lightning flashed back and forth. It was the worst storm in all the land of Egypt since it had become a nation. Throughout Egypt hail struck everything in the fields—both men and animals; it beat down everything growing in the fields and stripped every tree. (Exodus 9:22-25, NIV)

Where were Pharaoh's ace magicians in all this? They were out of the picture because they, too, had issues with the head-to-toe boils.

> And the magicians could not stand before Moses because of the boils, for the boils were on the magicians and on all the Egyptians. (Exodus 9:10)

The boils-and-hail one-two punch was just too much for Pharaoh. He finally showed signs of cracking.

> So Moses and Aaron were brought again to Pharaoh, and he said to them, "Go, serve the LORD your God. Who are the ones that are going?"

And Moses said, "We will go with our young and our old; with our sons and our daughters, with our flocks and our herds we will go, for we must hold a feast to the LORD."

Then he said to them, "The LORD had better be with you when I let you and your little ones go! Beware, for evil is ahead of you. Not so! Go now, you who are men, and serve the LORD, for that is what you desired." And they were driven out from Pharaoh's presence. (Exodus 10:8-11)

Pharaoh was willing to let them go, but…not with the kids. He knew that if they went to the wilderness while the children remained in Egypt, they'd come right back again. He would have them on a short leash.

Once again, however, God's man stood firm. Moses refused this compromise as well.

plagues 8 and 9: locusts and darkness

By the time the ninth plague rolled around, Pharaoh was ready for one final, desperate grasp at accommodation.

Then Pharaoh called to Moses and said, "Go, serve the LORD; only let your flocks and your herds be kept back. Let your little ones also go with you." (Exodus 10:24)

One more time, Pharaoh attempted to sound magnanimous. "Okay, go to the wilderness. Sacrifice to your God. And take your kids, since you insist on it. Just leave the animals behind."

Again, this is a picture of how our adversary, the Devil, will fight us tooth and nail for every inch of kingdom territory. He does not yield ground easily.

Why would Pharaoh care about their animals? Think of the progression here: First, he tried to keep the near the land. Next, he tried to get them to leave part of themselves in the land. And finally, he attempted to send them out without any sacrifices to offer to the Lord.

But Moses would have none of it. I love his response in verse 26: *"Not a hoof shall be left behind!"*

That's what we need to say to our adversary: Satan, you get nothing. Nada. Zip. Zero. You've ripped me off long enough, and I'm not going to give you so much as the time of day. *Get behind me!*

Are you trying to live the Christian life but toy with the dark side? Are you trying to keep one foot in both worlds?

Stop. Now. Before it's too late.

If Moses had compromised, he would have found himself outside the protection and power of God…and Pharaoh would have eaten him alive. And remember how Scripture describes our enemy: "Be careful! Watch out for attacks from the Devil, your great enemy. He prowls around like a roaring lion, looking for some victim to devour."

And the solution?

Take a firm stand against him, and be strong in your faith. Remember that your Christian brothers and sisters all over the world are going through the same kind of suffering you are. (1 Peter 5:8-9, NLT)

This is the only way to live a fruitful and successful life as a Christian. Otherwise, you will place yourself in a self-imposed wilderness of wandering, a miserable state of compromise…where you have "too much of the Lord to be happy with the world…and too much of the world to be happy with the Lord." You won't be able to enjoy fellowship with the Lord and His people, and you won't feel comfortable on the dark side, with Satan's people.

Standing on the barren top of Mount Carmel, silhouetted against the sky, the prophet Elijah challenged Israel, "Choose you this day whom you will serve."

We should respond like Joshua, who confronted his nation's compromises and said, "As for me and my house, we shall serve the LORD."

chapter eight

encounter at sinai, part 1: putting GOD first

thank God for absolutes.

In His wisdom and mercy, God has given us bedrock truths on which to build our lives, regardless of the shifting winds of modern culture. Those absolutes, standing strong and tall through the millennia, are the Ten Commandments.

It is my conviction that one of the reasons for the unprecedented blessings and great success of the United States of America over our 200 plus year history can be found in our origins, in the fact that our founding fathers built this country on a belief in Scripture and in the Ten Commandments.

James Madison, the man most responsible for the U.S. Constitution, wrote: "We have staked the whole future of American civilization, not upon the power of the government, far from it. We have staked the future of all our political constitutions upon the capacity of each and all of us to govern ourselves according to the Ten Commandments of God."

Abraham Lincoln said, "But for the Ten Commandments, we wouldn't know right from wrong."

That is certainly a far cry from where we are today. It seems like every time you turn around there's a new attempt to ban the commandments from public view, or remove every evidence of them from courtrooms, classrooms, and public squares.

It's ironic, because we desperately need to know and follow these commandments—not only for our personal survival, but for the survival of our nation. The fact is, we can either accept their truths, or fight against them and reap the inevitable results.

a lighthouse in the fog

Vance Havner said, "You cannot break the laws of God. You break yourself against them." Unfortunately, that is not the opinion of many today. Many of us don't like to be told what to do.

Consider the words Ted Turner, founder of CNN: "We're living with outmoded rules. The rules we're living under is the Ten Commandments, and I bet nobody here even pays much attention to 'em because they are too old. When Moses went up on the mountain, there were no nuclear weapons, there was no poverty. Today, the commandments wouldn't go over. Nobody around likes to be commanded. Commandments are out."

So what do we have in the place of the Ten Commandments? *Moral relativism.* It is the outright denial of any moral absolutes. In other words there is no right or wrong. It teaches that we are all products of the evolutionary process. There is no God, no plan, nor purpose for our lives. And Satan? Well, he's nothing more than a medieval myth.

Moral relativism teaches that we make our own luck or fate. We are all basically good inside, and if we go bad, it's because we are products of our environment. When it comes to truth, well, each of us has our own truth. The result is a life (or so they would like to think) of complete freedom from all restraint. And if you happen to disagree with this philosophy, holding on to a belief in right and wrong, you are an insensitive, intolerant, narrow-minded bigot! If you dare to quote the Bible, then you are imposing your puritanical value system. ("Cramming it down their throat"…have you heard that one before?)

Many of our young people are being raised with only the flimsiest of value systems. A recent article in the *Boston Globe* chronicled a phenomenon called "moral illiteracy" on America's college campuses. It started when William Kilpatrick, a professor of education at Boston College, began noticing what he would come to call signs of moral illiteracy among his students.

In one of his classes, they were discussing the Ten Commandments, and Professor Kilpatrick wanted to list them on the board. "It wasn't that individuals couldn't think of them all," he related later. "The whole class working together to come up with the complete list couldn't do it."

No wonder 67 percent of Americans say there is no such thing as right and wrong. A Barna report showed Generation X leading the way toward moral relativism. Born between 1965 and 1983, this generation rejected absolute truth by a staggering 78 percent.

I'm a chaplain with the police department, and recently attended a briefing on gang activity in our city. Here you have an entire sub-culture with their own values, rules, and beliefs.

I asked what the solution was.

The officer in charge said, "It has to happen in the home."

The cure for crime is not in the electric chair but in the high chair, laying a godly foundation for our children and their children. It's time to get back to God's unchanging absolutes. It's time to go back to the Ten Commandments. They are straight forward, concise, to the point—a clear grid to live by. In a culture where morality has been lost in the fog, the Ten Commandments are like the bright beam from a lighthouse, showing us right from wrong, good from evil, true from false, up from down—and warning lost and disoriented lives away from the rocks.

After wasting his life and unimaginable potential, Solomon wrote these words at the close of the book of Ecclesiastes: "Now all has been heard; here is the conclusion of the matter: Fear God and keep his commandments, for this is the whole duty of man."[36]

The whole duty of man. That's another way of saying that if a man or woman keeps God's commandments, he or she will be a whole person. Solomon himself had violated many of these commands and knew what he spoke of.

For instance, when he said, "Nothing my eyes desired did I keep from them," it was a direct violation of the tenth commandment: *"You shall not covet."* When he stated, "I had concubines," he was living in opposition to the seventh commandment: *"You shall not commit adultery."* As an old man looking back on his failures and tragic decisions, Solomon is saying, "If you violate these—if you turn your back on God's commandments—your life will be out of balance. And you will be the great loser."

meanwhile, back at mount sinai...

When we last left Moses he was demanding the release of the Israelites from a persistently hard-hearted Pharaoh. Finally—and with great reluctance—the Pharaoh agreed…only to change his mind again and set off in hot pursuit.

When they stood at the brink of the Red Sea, God opened up a path through its midst for Israel to cross on dry land—but closed it back on the pursuing Egyptian armies. As they advanced through the wilderness, the Lord led His people with a cloud by day and a pillar of fire by night. Each and every day He had manna waiting for them to sustain them on their journey.

Now they have come to Mount Sinai, and God instructs Moses to ascend, while the people remain behind, and wait for God's Word. Up in that awesome, frightening cloud at the top of the mountain, God began to deliver His Ten Commandments to His servant.

And God spoke all these words, saying:

"I am the LORD your God, who brought you out of the land of Egypt, out of the house of bondage.

"You shall have no other gods before Me.

"You shall not make for yourself a carved image—any likeness of anything that is in heaven above, or that is in the earth beneath, or that is in the water under the earth; you shall not bow down to them nor serve them. For I, the LORD your God, am a jealous God, visiting the iniquity of the fathers upon the children to the third and fourth generations of those who hate Me, but showing mercy to thousands, to those who love Me and keep

My commandments.

"You shall not take the name of the LORD your God in vain, for the LORD will not hold him guiltless who takes His name in vain.

"Remember the Sabbath day, to keep it holy. Six days you shall labor and do all your work, but the seventh day is the Sabbath of the LORD your God. In it you shall do no work: you, nor your son, nor your daughter, nor your male servant, nor your female servant, nor your cattle, nor your stranger who is within your gates. For in six days the LORD made the heavens and the earth, the sea, and all that is in them, and rested the seventh day. Therefore the LORD blessed the Sabbath day and hallowed it.

"Honor your father and your mother, that your days may be long upon the land which the LORD your God is giving you.

"You shall not murder.

"You shall not commit adultery.

"You shall not steal.

"You shall not bear false witness against your neighbor.

"You shall not covet your neighbor's house; you shall not covet your neighbor's wife, nor his male servant, nor his female servant, nor his ox, nor his donkey, nor anything that is your neighbor's." (Exodus 20:1-7)

If you and I set out to reorganize the Ten Commandments, we might list them differently, moving murder or adultery to the top of the list. Surely, "Having another God before Him" is not as serious as *those* sins.

But for God, breaking commandment Number One is the Number One offense. In the eyes of heaven, there is nothing worse than putting another god before the true and living One.

One day a man came to Jesus and asked Him, "What is the greatest commandment?"

Jesus answered him, "The first of all the commandments is: 'Hear, O Israel, the LORD our God, the LORD is one. And you shall love the LORD your God with all your heart, with all your soul, with all your mind, and with all your strength.' This is the first commandment. And the second, like it, is this: 'You shall love your neighbor as yourself.' There is no other commandment greater than these." (Mark 12:29-31)

With that statement Jesus really sums up the Ten Commandments. "Have no other gods before Me" is *the first of all.* It's also the one most of us don't think we ever break. A survey revealed that 76 percent of all Americans consider themselves completely faithful to the first commandment.

Is that true? Have most Americans avoided placing another "god" in the place of the God of the Bible?

I doubt that. But let's check it out...let's take a closer look at the implications of that primary command.

dealing with numero uno

It all starts with the place of God in your life.

Why? *Because you will serve who or what you worship.* Jesus said, "You shall worship the Lord your God, Him only shall you serve." If God is Who He says He is, then He deserves our undivided attention. If the Lord is Number One in your life, everything and everyone else will find its proper balance. But if He's not in first place, everything else will be in chaos. Note the wording that the Lord uses here in Exodus 20:2:

"I am the LORD your God, who brought you out of the land of Egypt, out of the house of bondage."

It's amazing how much can be revealed by a simple little word such as "I." This little pronoun, only one letter long, conveys a profound and fundamental truth about who God is. As James Kennedy points out, when He said, "I am the Lord," He is refuting all other belief systems—including pantheism, polytheism, deism, and New Age thinking.[37]

When Moses stood before the burning bush out in the desert, God declared the essence of His identity: "I AM WHO I AM…Thus you shall say to the children of Israel, 'I AM has sent me to you.'"[38]

When God said "I Am," He revealed that He is a person. He was in essence saying, "I am, I feel, I act." God is not, as pantheism teaches, an impersonal force.

Pantheism alleges that All is God, the universe is God, everything is God. Plants. Trees. Rocks. Bugs. You name it. But the Lord says, "I am the LORD, and there is no other; there is no God besides Me" (Isaiah 45:5).

Polytheism—such as practiced by Hindus—believes in many gods. But God didn't say "We are the Lord, your gods." He said, "I am the Lord, your God." As Paul said so clearly to Timothy, "For there is one God and one Mediator between God and men, the Man Christ Jesus, who gave Himself a ransom for all."[39]

Deism proposes that God created the world, wound it up like a clock, then went off and forgot all about it. Deists would say that God has no interest in the affairs of men. But the Bible clearly reveals a God who sees, hears, and cares. And this same God, *Yahweh*—who led, protected, and blessed His people—still wants to do that today for us.

New Age thinking claims that the answer is inside of you. You are God. New Age thinking is nothing but the original lie of Satan recycled for our times in hip, politically correct terminology. In the Garden, remember, the Evil One said to Eve, "You shall be as gods….." Malcolm Muggeridge has aptly noted that "all new news is old news happening to new people."

Today, we have substituted religion for faith, and "spirituality" for godliness. *Spirituality.* That's clearly the buzzword of the day. "I'm not into organized religion," people will tell you, "I'm simply a spiritual person."

As a culture, we want to have our cake and eat it, too. We want a belief system, but one that doesn't get in our way or place boundaries on our lives. As you might imagine, there all sorts of leaders and proponents willing to step forward for this "new and improved spirituality."

In contrast to all of that, we have God's bedrock truth in these commandments—inscribed by His very finger.

In the preamble to the Ten Commandments, God reminds the Israelites of what He had already done for them. How He had so graciously answered their prayers and demonstrated His love. How He brought them from a miserable life of slavery and delivered them.

This is the God who gives them basic rules for living. He doesn't start by threatening or scaring them. He starts by reminding them of what kind of God He is: A loving, caring God who rescued them from captivity and a hopeless future.

Well, that's great for *them*, you might say. But I've never been a slave in Egypt. True…yet you were a slave to sin on your way to Hell. But God loved you so much He sent His son Jesus to die on the cross in your place. Now if we really appreciate what He has done, if we know anything of His all-encompassing forgiveness, it should be our privilege and pleasure to live a life pleasing to Him. Not because we have to but because we want to! *We love Him because He first loved us.*

commandments 1 and 2: "no other gods, no idols"

What does it mean to have another god before Him?

In many places in the world, you can still see grotesque idols carved from wood or stone, and people bowing down to them and worshiping them. But in America? That's not something we see very often—even in Southern California, where I live.

The truth is, "other gods" covers a lot more territory than that.

An idol is anything or anyone that takes the place of God in our lives. And know this, *everybody has a God.* Even atheists have a god. They might call it "knowledge" or "human reason" or "science," but it is their god, nonetheless, and one whom they worship and serve.

The question is: who or what is your God? What gets you excited? What gets you out of bed in the morning? What do you think about most? What do you dream about, plan for, perhaps scheme for. What are you really passionate about?

That is your God.

Now most people reading this book would say, "The Lord is my God." Maybe He is. Then again, maybe He isn't. Our God isn't just One we might name, He is One whom we serve.

What is the focus of your life? Is it your career, your family? That, for all practical purposes, becomes your God.

Once again, the Second Commandment says: "You shall not make for yourself a carved image…you shall not bow down to them nor serve them."

You wonder, how could this happen? How did Israel end up throwing God over so quickly and worshiping the Golden Calf? It happens easier than you may think.

There were two phases to the Israelites' idolatry in Exodus 32: the first more subtle and less obvious, the second blatantly radical. And the first phase will always grow out of the other. The root of their open idolatry was the previous departure of their hearts from the Lord, leaning too much on the man who was God's chosen instrument and spokesman. *Moses.*

"let's lower the bar a little…"

Moses was their first idol, the Golden Calf their second. After Moses disappeared into the cloud on top of Mount Sinai for weeks on end, they started getting restless. Their "idol" was out of sight, so what were they to do?

> When Moses failed to come back down the mountain right away, the people went to Aaron. "Look," they said, "make us some gods who can lead us. This man Moses, who brought us here from Egypt, has disappeared. We don't know what has happened to him." (Exodus 32:1, NLT)

They were essentially saying, "We don't know about Moses anymore. Anyway, his standards were awfully high. We still want 'spirituality,' but let's just lower the bar a little. Let's create something we can see and touch, something which appeals to the senses. We don't want to feel guilty if we don't do what God says. So let's just make up our own version.

What's wrong with that? How would you like it if an airline pilot said something similar? "I'm sick of all these charts and buttons and lights, constantly worrying if we have enough fuel. Let's just go with the flow, man!" Or what if a surgeon picked up that line of reasoning? "Who cares about all these extra arteries all over the place! They're just in the way! Just give me a scalpel and I'll figure it out as I go!"

What if one individual decided that traffic laws didn't really apply to him? "Hey man, that's your truth, and that's good for you. I've got my own truth." So he decides that a red light means go, and a green light means stop, and the sign that says "yield" really means "go for it."

Is it any more ridiculous when people try to give God a twenty-first century makeover? You can say, "The Bible says God is a jealous God. But I don't want Him to be jealous. I want Him to be mellow and laid back. I want Him to be tolerant and adaptable. So that's the God I'm going to worship." Or maybe, "I know the Bible says Jesus is the only way to God, but I don't believe in judgment. I believe in a God who accepts everybody no matter what."

Statements like those go directly against the first and foremost of the Ten Commandments. By creating your own version of God, you are placing another god before the true God.

The Israelites rationalized it, of course. They called partying before the Golden Calf "a festival to the Lord." In a similar way, you may be out all night breaking the commands of God, but say grace before a meal. As if that will somehow satisfy God or make what you are doing acceptable. Or you pray "ten Hail Mary's" and five "Our Fathers," and everything is ok with God.

What the Israelites were doing would be like saying, "Lord, bless this night as we get drunk and commit fornication." God doesn't want us bowing before images *period*.

With idolatry all around them in Egypt, it may have been difficult for the Israelites to get used to the idea of worshiping an invisible God. And it may not be easy for us sometimes, either. Even so, Jesus said, "God is Spirit, and those who worship Him must worship in spirit and truth."[40]

Why, then, do we have people bowing before statues of saints, or an image of Jesus on the cross? Well, they might reply, it helps them to relate to God because it's something they can actually see.

Listen! A person who really knows God, who's experienced the new birth and is living in fellowship with Him, doesn't *need* an image or representation to help him pray. God becomes very real to the individual who is filled with the Holy Spirit and walking daily with Jesus Christ. You don't need a physical reminder.

This is not to say that a painting or representation of Jesus is necessarily wrong. It's most likely inaccurate, but it's not bad in and of itself. But it is wrong—terribly wrong—when bit by bit the image begins to take the place of God. It is violating the Second Commandment.

The crucifix is a good example. It's meant as a reminder of the fact that Jesus suffered and died on the cross. But some people carry them as good luck charms, thinking that the little cross will somehow fend off evil. It becomes a holy object to them. The same is true of a statue of Jesus. You bow before it, saying it represents the Lord to you. But doesn't that look a lot like bowing before a graven image?

If it walks like a duck, and quacks like a duck, I think it is one.

Imagine I'm returning from a long ministry trip, and my wife Cathe meets me at the airport. Now, I usually try to carry a photo of my wife in my wallet. But how would Cathe feel if when I saw her, I stopped short, pulled out that photo and began kissing it—instead of her! Someone would probably call the guys in the white coats to take me away.

Why kiss a picture when the real deal is right in front of me? And why bow before an image, picture, or symbol when the real God is there for you?

The same thing can even happen with a Bible. Some people won't set another book on top of the Bible. Others are shocked when they see people writing notes on its pages. Not me! I like to see a Bible all beat up, with dog-eared pages and a worn cover. That shows it's been used. A Bible that's falling apart probably belongs to someone who isn't.

We cannot create anything that will ever be a true representation of the living God. Why? Because it will give us a false concept of what God is really like. If the image is false, the thought of God is false, and that produces character which is false.

Speaking of idols, the psalmist wrote:

They have mouths, but they do not speak;
Eyes they have, but they do not see;
They have ears, but they do not hear;
Noses they have, but they do not smell;
They have hands, but they do not handle;
Feet they have, but they do not walk;
Nor do they mutter through their throat.
Those who make them are like them;
So is everyone who trusts in them.
(Psalm 115:5-8)

A man becomes like the thing he worships. If he puts anything in the place of God, he ultimately becomes like it. After all, what does it mean to be a Christian? It is to become like Jesus.

"Dear children," the elderly apostle John wrote, *"keep away from anything that might take God's place in your hearts"* (1 John 5:21, TLB). Is the Lord Number One in your life today? Are you allowing other gods to crowd Him out?

Remember, Jesus brought all the commandments into context when He said, "'You shall love the LORD your God with all your heart, with all your soul, with all your mind, and with all your strength.' This is the first commandment. And the second,

like it, is this: 'You shall love your neighbor as yourself.'
There is no other commandment greater than these."

With that statement Jesus really sums up the Ten
Commandments. The first four relate to my relationship
with God; the second six relate to my relationship to others.

Numbers 1 through 4 teach love for God.
Numbers 5 through 10 teach love for others.
Numbers 1 through 4 are vertical.
Numbers 5 through 10 are horizontal.

If I truly love God, I will not have other gods before Him,
bow before graven images, or take His name in vain. If I truly
love my neighbor as myself, I won't steal from him, lie to him,
covet what is his, or kill him.

But going back to the First Commandment, we all need to
be very careful to make sure that God truly is Number One in
our hearts and lives. It is deceptively easy to *say* you worship
the Lord, yet allow your heart to be captured by other "gods."

some worship money or possessions

Their mantra is "born to shop," or "he who dies with the most
toys wins." Of course the great difficulty here is that once you
get what you want, you soon tire of it and want more!

Hell and Destruction are never full;
So the eyes of man are never satisfied.
(Proverbs 27:20)

When John D. Rockefeller was the richest man in the world,
someone asked him, "How much money is enough."

He replied, "Just a little bit more".

The Bible warns us saying, "The love of money is a root of all
kinds of evil. Some people, eager for money, have wandered from
the faith and pierced themselves with many griefs."[41]

Those people "eager for money" in the above passage may
squander the little cash they have gambling, buying lotto tickets.
They tell themselves that if they could only win "Who Wants To

Be A Millionaire," they would finally find a little happiness. If we learn nothing else from those who have been successful in Hollywood, surely we have seen the emptiness of merely possessing things. How many of these people are on drugs, in rehab, miserable, and empty?

Jesus said, "What will it profit a man if he gains the whole world, and loses his own soul? Or what will a man give in exchange for his soul?" (Mark 8:36-38).

This was the case with the rich young ruler. He had it all: he was wealthy, young, even moral…but still empty inside. Jesus told him to sell all he had and give it to the poor, and he went away sorrowful. His God was the *stuff* that kept him from the living Savior who loved him.

some worship their own bodies

They worship at the First Church of the Perfect Physique. There is never quite enough exercise, weight lifting, running, or whatever. It can become addicting. Doesn't it drive you crazy when someone who looks like they're in perfect shape say, "Oh, I can't eat that, I'm getting so fat."

Have you seen how more and more people seem to be turning to cosmetic surgeons. People are getting just a little carried away. I saw a piece on TV not long ago about two girls who wanted to look exactly like Barbie. Another woman wanted to look like a *cat!*

some worship pleasure

I say it again now with tears in my eyes, there are many who walk along the Christian road who are really enemies of the cross of Christ. Their future is eternal loss, for their god is their appetite: they are proud of what they should be ashamed of; and all they think about is this life here on earth. (Philippians 3:18-9, TLB)

You know people like this. They live for that buzz, that experience, that thrill. The Bible says, "In the last days perilous times will come: For men will be…lovers of pleasure rather than lovers of God."[42]

Some just live for the moment. For what excites them. For many this might involve putting their whole focus on sensual or sexual pleasure. The problem with this is that once you've tried one thing, you soon tire of it and want more. Or "different." The unrestrained sensual appetite invariably becomes more perverse, deviant, and twisted. An unholy sensual desire cannot be satisfied legitimately.

Sadly, we could all think of some graphic examples of that, and yet Scripture tells us that it's "shameful even to speak of those things which are done by them in secret."[43]

Living for pleasure is a dead-end street. As Paul wrote, "She who lives in pleasure is dead while she lives."[44]

I'm amazed by the length the Holy Spirit goes to in order to keep us off this road of destruction. The life of Solomon has been captured for us in Scripture, so that we won't have to run down every heartbreaking dead-end street that he did. And when you read the following passage, you'll realize he ran down just about all of them.

> I also tried to find meaning by building huge homes for myself and by planting beautiful vineyards. I made gardens and parks, filling them with all kinds of fruit trees. I built reservoirs to collect the water to irrigate my many flourishing groves. I bought slaves, both men and women, and others were born into my household. I also owned great herds and flocks, more than any of the kings who lived in Jerusalem before me. I collected great sums of silver and gold, the treasure of many kings and provinces. I hired wonderful singers, both men and women, and had many beautiful concubines. I had everything a man could desire!

So I became greater than any of the kings who ruled in Jerusalem before me. And with it all, I remained clear-eyed so that I could evaluate all these things. Anything I wanted, I took. I did not restrain myself from any joy. I even found great pleasure in hard work, an additional reward for all my labors. But as I looked at everything I had worked so hard to accomplish, it was all so meaningless. It was like chasing the wind. There was nothing really worthwhile anywhere. (Ecclesiastes 2:4-11, NLT)

After all of that…after unlimited job opportunities…unlimited wealth…unlimited creative fulfillment…unlimited sensual pleasure, Solomon sums it up by saying, in essence, "It was all a big zero. I've wasted my life."

You see, that's why Solomon said at the end of Ecclesiastics, "This is the end of the matter, all has been heard. Fear God and keep His commandments, for this is the whole of man."

This is the whole of man, and this is what makes man whole.

Of Moses it was said, "He chose to be mistreated along with the people of God rather than to enjoy the pleasures of sin for a short time" (Hebrews 11:25, NIV).

When Jesus met the woman at the well in Samaria, He knew that she had spent her life trying to fill the void inside with romance, sex, men. He said to her, "If you drink of this water you will thirst again…."

That is true of common well water…and possessions, pleasure, the perfect body, and everything else out there that would try to fill the vacuum in our soul meant for God alone.

some worship people

At one time or another, we've probably all referred to a certain actor or musician as our "idol." We want to be just like them. Or it could even be a godly man or woman we admire and want to emulate. The problem with idols—all idols—is that they will invariably disappoint you. You can make an idol or god out of a boyfriend, girlfriend, a gang, whatever. This person or these people become more important to you than God Himself. This is shown by the fact that you will do anything to keep your relationship with these people—*even deny the Lord and abandon your faith.*

It happens all the time. "If I really give my life to Jesus Christ I might lose this person…."

Yes, you might.

Jesus said, "If anyone comes to Me and does not hate his father and mother, wife and children, brothers and sisters, yes, and his own life also, he cannot be My disciple."[45]

The fact is, everything about this world is changing. Even the people we love most will one day pass away. The only real security in this whole universe is in our eternal God.

Thank God for absolutes! Thank God that His Word never changes… and neither does His love.

chapter nine

encounter at sinai, part 2: finding the road to happiness

are you a happy person?
You may have all the things a person ought to have to make them happy and content, and yet…you're not.

Why is that?

Because there is a right and wrong way to find happiness. There are two ways we can live in life, two paths we can take. Jesus says there is narrow way that leads to life, and the broad way that leads to destruction.

There are two foundations on which we can build: the rock, or the sinking sand. And the result is we can either live the happy and holy way or the miserable and unholy way.

When most people think of that narrow way, the life of obedience to God, they foresee misery, restrictions, and rules, rules, rules. The picture most non-believing people have of the Christian is one of gloom, pessimism, and—worst of all— extreme boredom. No drinking, smoking, partying, or sex (at least outside of marriage). In essence, *no fun!* Instead, they imagine every spare hour spent in Bible studies, prayer, or hanging out with other dull people.

In fact, the very opposite is true.

Jesus told the story of a young man who ran away from home—and it was a picture of what happens when we run away from God.[46] Have you ever noticed that the prodigal son found everything he was looking for in his father's house? What did he look for in the prodigal land to make him happy? Apparently nice clothes, fine food, and parties. Yet what did his father give to the rebellious son when he returned? Nice clothes, *bring out the best robe.* Fine food, *bring out the fatted calf.* And parties, *let's be merry!*

Everything that he needed in life he ultimately found in his father's house. And everything we need in life to make us truly happy is found there, too, in the realm of our heavenly Father.

You hear people talk about "what they gave up" to follow Christ, but honestly, what have they really lost? Addiction to drugs or alcohol? Hangovers? Unhappy, unhealthy relationships? Guilt? Emptiness? Fear of death?

Paul said, "Everything else is worthless when compared with the priceless gain of knowing Christ Jesus my Lord. I have put aside all else, counting it worth less than nothing, in order that I can have Christ" (Philippians 3:8, TLB)

The word "blessed" that we see so often in the Bible actually means "happy." Literally, it means *happy, happy!* But where are we to find this double-happy state the Bible promises? By doing what God tells us to do.

The psalmist wrote: "Blessed is the man who fears the LORD, who delights greatly in His commandments" (Psalm 112:1). In other words, "Happy, happy the man or woman who takes great delights in the commandments of God."

Happiness is always connected to holiness. That's why the non-believer will never know true happiness. Sure, they will have moments of temporary happiness, but it will be short-lived. The Devil has his cheap counterfeits, but they are shallow because they have no deep well from which to draw. Our holy God, however, is the very headwaters of joy.

Ironically, you'll find that the most unhappy people are the people living for happiness! Happiness isn't something that we should seek outright, as an end in itself, it is a *by-product* of seeking and serving God. Happiness sneaks up on you when you're not looking as you seek to follow Christ and help people in His name. As Christians, we should not seek to be happy, we should seek to be holy—and we'll find happiness thrown into the bargain.

Psalm 1 says:

Blessed [happy, happy] is the man
Who walks not in the counsel of the ungodly,
Nor stands in the path of sinners,
Nor sits in the seat of the scornful;
But his delight is in the law of the Lord….
(vv. 1-2)

Happy-twice-over is the man who *walks not*…. His happiness isn't springing from what he does, but what he chooses not to do! The Ten Commandments aren't bars of a cage to keep us in, as much as they are barriers to keep evil out. Have you ever seen those underwater photographers who are lowered in cages into a shark-infested sea? Do you think their dominant emotion is frustration over being "hemmed in"? I doubt it! I think they are probably thanking God for the protection.

The Ten Commandments, remember, can be divided into two sections. The first four deal with my relationship with God, and the next six with my relationship with man. When we love God with all our heart, soul, and mind, we will be better able to love our neighbor as ourselves.

We have already looked at the first two commandments. For the next few pages, we'll be considering the third.

commandment 3: don't take his name in vain

Here is one of the most misunderstood of the commandments— and one which can so easily be broken. How do we take His name in vain?

1. through profanity

God's last name is not "damn." It's always been curious to me how many who claim to be atheists invoke the name of God and Jesus so often. Even the non-believer, in his spiritually deadened state knows there is something different, something powerful, something special about invoking the name of God or the name of Jesus Christ.

The Bible makes it very clear that that there is no higher, more honored, more powerful name in all of the universe.

> Therefore God also has highly exalted Him and given Him the name which is above every name, that at the name of Jesus every knee should bow, of those in heaven, and of those on earth, and of those under the earth, and that every tongue should confess that Jesus Christ is Lord, to the glory of God the Father. (Philippians 2:9-11)

God's name is important to Him.

Names are important to us, too.

Parents anguish over what name to give their child. At this writing, the five most popular names for girls at this writing are: Emma, Madison, Emily, Kaitlyn and Hailey. (Whatever happened to Debby, Sandy, Carol, or Susie?) Stone or gem names are hot choices for girls, leading to names such as Amber, Jade, Diamond, and of course, Crystal. The five most popular names for boys are: Jacob, Aidan, Ethan, Ryan, Matthew, and…Greg Laurie! (Just kidding.) Geographic names are also popular for boys, like Austin, Dakota, Zaire, Dallas, Sky, and Ridge.

Then there are those parents who think it's clever to stick their kids with a name that is a humorous play on words. These names are for real: Paige Turner, Warren Piece, Justin Case, Carl Arm, Chris B. Bacon, Eileen Dover, Gene Pool, Douglas Fir, and Cookie Cutter.

Names are important to God, too, especially His own name. God is very, very serious about His name. We have laws against slandering someone's personal name, and you can be taken to court for that offence. In the same way, there is a penalty for those who hold God's name in contempt and drag it through the mud. The Bible says, "For the LORD will not hold him guiltless who takes His name in vain."[47]

This is no idle threat, it's simply a statement of fact. God is setting forth an unchanging truth, something that's hardwired into Creation, not unlike the Law of Gravity. If you step off a thirty story building, you will fall to your death. That's not a threat, it's simply a statement of fact, a statement of *what is*. In the same way, if you take God's name in vain, you will not be held guiltless or go unpunished.

I shudder when I hear people go out of their way to insult or blaspheme God. The Bible tells us, "Do not be deceived, God is not mocked; for whatever a man sows, that he will also reap."[48]

We must never forget the holiness of our God. It is one of the most important, most repeated facts in all of Scripture. The angels around His throne do not say, "Eternal, eternal, eternal," or "faithful, faithful, faithful," or "mighty, mighty, mighty" (though He is all of those things). What they say is "Holy, holy, holy is the Lord God Almighty—the one who always was, who is, and who is still to come."[49]

So we want to always have reverence and respect for His holy name. What are some other ways that we take His name in vain?

2. through needless oaths

Sometimes we may say, "I swear to God this is true…."

Okay, so it's true. But why do we have to bring God into it?

Probably because our word is not normally reliable. People who make commitments they don't keep or say things that aren't true think that by invoking the name of God, their promise will have more credibility. So we drag God's honor into the conversation to try to buttress our own. Jesus spoke directly to this practice in His Sermon on the Mount.

> "Again, you have heard that it was said to the people long ago, 'Do not break your oath, but keep the oaths you have made to the Lord.' But I tell you, Do not swear at all: either by heaven, for it is God's throne; or by the earth, for it is his footstool; or by Jerusalem, for it is the city of the Great King. And do not swear by your head, for you cannot make even one hair white or black. Simply let your 'Yes' be 'Yes,' and your 'No,' 'No'; anything beyond this comes from the evil one." (Matthew 5:33-37, NIV)

Don't bring God or heaven into your promises. Your word should be enough. To strengthen your promise with a vow shows that you have a credibility problem, and need to take steps to change that. What kind of steps? Let me list a few.

First, if you say that you're going to do something, *do it!* Don't make commitments you don't intend to keep. Don't say, "Oh sure, we'll meet you for dinner," and then cancel at the last minute because someone you like better called. Watch out! You may go out to dinner with the second person who called and then bump into the person you cancelled!

Don't say, "Oh yeah, I'll help you move out of your house this weekend," and then neglect to show up and call later with an excuse. We have a word for people who do things like these: *flakes.*

Second, if you're hired to do a job, do it. Get it done. Christians should be the hardest-working, and most diligent workers, and we should never use our faith as an excuse for laziness. ("I can't sweep the floor now, I need to *pray.*")

Third, when two people commit themselves to each other in marriage, they should honor those vows for the rest of their lives. People today—even Christians—follow the trend of our times and just bail out of a marriage when it gets hard. They will cite "irreconcilable differences."

Jesus says, "Don't be like that." Let your yes be yes and your no, no.

3. by using his name for personal gain

Then there are those who misuse His name to further their business transactions. You can look in the Yellow Pages and see the sign of the fish on ads for car dealers, landscaping services, and Realtors.

Sadly, it goes much, much further than that. We have many people today involved in what is called "Christian retailing," who essentially market Christian products. You can purchase a Christian version of just about anything out there.

At what used to be called the CBA, or the Christian Booksellers Association conventions, you'll find everything from outstanding Christian books and music to ashtrays and lighters with the holy name of Jesus emblazoned them. You can get Christian bird feeders, body lotions, luggage, lamps, scones, mud flaps, wallpaper, candy bars, Frisbees, and mouse pads.

Do I have to have Christian mud flaps to be spiritual? Or Christian luggage? If you ask me, some of this is taking the Lord's name in vain. They are exploiting the name of Jesus to make a buck.

4. by being flippant or careless

It is possible that even sincere believers take His name in vain, without intending to. The phrase "in vain" describes that which is empty, idle, insincere, or frivolous. God's name must never be used in an empty, frivolous, or insincere way. When we say, "God bless you," "Praise the Lord," "Hallelujah," or "I'll pray for you," let those be heartfelt, sincere statements, not empty clichés.

The J. B. Phillips paraphrase of Romans 12:9 says, "Let us have no imitation Christian love." Another translation says, "Don't just pretend that you love others. Really love them."[50]

Perhaps the most subtle form in which this law is broken is by sheer hypocrisy: The man who claims Jesus as Lord but does not keep His commandments. Jesus said, "Why do you call Me 'Lord, Lord,' and not do the things which I say?" (Luke 6:46).

I'm going to make a statement that might shock you, but I believe it to be true: *The hypocrisy of the church is far worse than the profanity in the street.* To pray and not to practice, to believe and not to obey, to say, "Lord, Lord," and not do what He says…this is to take His holy name in vain! Now we come to the Fourth Commandment.

commandment 4:
remember the sabbath day

This command has produced more confusion, misunderstanding, and hard feelings than perhaps any of the others. Let's find out what it is…and what it *isn't*.

The original context of this command, of course, was a word to the Israelites, instructing them to set aside the seventh day as a day of total rest.

And now I'll make another statement that may shock you (two in one chapter): This command doesn't mean much for Christians living under grace. Let me tell you why I believe this. Here are some fast facts about the Fourth Commandment.

it is the only commandment not repeated in the new testament

Every one of the other Ten Commandments is repeated in the pages of the New Testament, and most are made more stringent. However, in all the New Testament lists of sins, breaking the Sabbath is never mentioned. Why? Because it was given to the Jews, not the non-Jews.

JESUS never taught anyone to keep the sabbath

Jesus actually broke the Sabbath Law as it was followed in His day (Matthew 12:1-14). By perverting and twisting the meaning of the Sabbath, the Jewish leaders had turned it into a miserable, religious mess. Because Jesus healed people and made them whole on the Sabbath day they accused Him of breaking it! That's when He reminded them that man was not made for the Sabbath, but the Sabbath for man.

It's sad how religion takes the place of a relationship with God. It becomes all about going through rituals and rules with no real thought of a relationship with God Himself.

the apostles never taught anyone to keep the sabbath.

In fact, they deliberately began meeting on the first day of the week, Sunday, because Jesus rose on Sunday. They spoke against turning the Sabbath into a religious law for Christians. Paul taught specifically on this subject:

So don't let anyone condemn you for what you eat or drink, or for not celebrating certain holy days or new-moon ceremonies or Sabbaths. For these rules were only shadows of the real thing, Christ himself. (Colossians 2:16-17, NLT)

The apostle pointed out that all the Sabbath had been pointing to in the Old Testament scrolls was fulfilled in Jesus Christ!

The book of Hebrews underlines this wonderful truth:

So there is a special rest still waiting for the people of God. For all who enter into God's rest will find rest from their labors, just as God rested after creating the world. Let us do our best to enter that place of rest. For anyone who disobeys God, as the people of Israel did, will fall. (Hebrews 4:9-11, NLT)

Other religions teaching on salvation say "Do," while Jesus Christ says *"Done."* [51] I am not under command to keep just one day special for the Lord, any more than I am required to approach God by means of animal sacrifices. There is no need! Those were signposts pointing me to Jesus, and full salvation in Him.

Knowing then, what the Sabbath is not, does it have any message to us as Christians? I believe there are two primary purposes behind the Sabbath principle.

a day of rest

The Sabbath was to be a day of rest. God wants us to know that we need at least one day off out of seven to rest and recharge. Most of us are in a hurry. Have you noticed that life moves faster every day? We are the only nation in the world with a mountain called *Rushmore.* Many of us live constantly on the edge, our schedules jam-packed. And suddenly one day we wonder how so much of life passed us by!

We keep trying to cram more living into increasingly limited lives. That's the life principle behind the Fourth Commandment, we need *rest.* Our homes are filled with labor saving devices intended to make our lives easier than ever, and yet we have never worked harder. No wonder we're stressed out! We need a day to unplug the computer, turn off the cell phone, and *chill*.

As I quoted earlier in the book, the Lord says, "Be still and know that I am God."[52] Most of us can quote that verse—or even write it in calligraphy and frame it on the walls of our home. But it has to move beyond nice words into a definite, disciplined plan of action. We *need* to be still sometimes. God speaks to us in the stillness. David spoke of how the Lord led him into green pastures by still waters…and restored his soul. If we want the restoration, we have to be willing to walk with Him into the quiet place and sit down for awhile.

Even Jesus took time off.

> The apostles gathered around Jesus and reported to him all they had done and taught. Then, because so many people were coming and going that they did not even have a chance to eat, he said to them, "Come with me by yourselves to a quiet place and get some rest." So they went away by themselves in a boat to a solitary place. (Mark 6:30-32, NIV)

Our emphasis always seems to be on doing, but God is interested in our rest. He knows we need it. During the next 24 hours let me show you how hard your body will work. Your heart beats 103,689 times, your blood travels 168,000,000 miles, you breathe 23,040 times, you inhale 438 cubic feet of air, you eat 3 and a half pounds of food, you drink 2.9 quarts of liquid. You speak 4,800 words (that's one phone call for most girls!). You move 750 muscles, and you exercise 7,000,000 brain cells.

Whew! I feel tired just writing this stuff. We need a day to rest our bodies and be recharged spiritually. For many, Sunday is that day. Sunday is not the Sabbath, but a good day to honor the principle. It can be a time to get together with God's people to worship, pray, look at Scripture, and enjoy each other's company.

This is not an "option" for a believer, it's a *necessity*. If you fail to do this you will soon become a casualty in the race of life.

Now that we've considered the first four commandments covering our vertical relationship with the Lord, we need to shift gears to look at the following six commandments, speaking to our horizontal relationships with one another.

commandment 5: honor your father and mother

Before a word is spoken about how you treat others, God starts with the family. Few things can give us as much pleasure in life as our families. Then again, few things can give us as much *pain* in life as our families.

Kids have problems with parents, parents have problems with kids. Husbands have trouble with wives, and wives have trouble with husbands. But God starts with the family because He created it.

In fact, our very existence as a society is contingent on the success of the family. That's probably why Satan hates it so, and has declared war on families all over the world.

Tragically, in today's twisted times, mothers and fathers aren't even around to honor—especially fathers. A man and a woman, married faithfully and raising their children is becoming less and less the norm. Currently, one million teenagers—12 percent of all women ages 15 and 19—become pregnant each year. Of those, 70 percent are unmarried. *The New York Times* has reported that unmarried pregnant teenagers are beginning to be viewed by some of their peers as role models. Research has found that a majority of Americans agree that single mothers can raise children as well as married couples.

They *can't*. Not even close.

And 70 percent of Americans between ages 18 and 34 think having children outside of marriage is "morally acceptable."

It *isn't*. It is neither moral nor acceptable, and it breaks the heart of the God who created marriage.

It has even come into vogue in Hollywood for actresses to have kids out of wedlock. They are the "new, liberated people."

Then you have homosexuals adopting kids—so incalculably destructive to God's order. God says, honor your father and mother—not honor your father and father or honor your mother and her live-in lover or partner. We tamper with God's order at our own peril!

Consider these statistics: 70 percent of juveniles in state–operated institutions come from fatherless homes; 63 percent of youth suicides are from fatherless homes; 90 percent of homeless and runaway children are from fatherless homes.

The Hebrew in this command for honoring your mom and dad comes from a verb *to be heavy,* or *to give weight.*

> Children, obey your parents in all things, for this is well pleasing to the Lord. (Colossians 3:20)

Respect for parents is certainly something we have lost sight of in our culture. It's interesting that one of the signs of the last days will be a lack of respect for one's parents. Paul tells Timothy, "For men will be lovers of themselves, lovers of money, boasters, proud, blasphemers, disobedient to parents…." (2 Timothy 3:2).

You might say, "Greg, my mom and dad aren't even Christians. Should I still honor them?" *Yes.* In fact, in doing so you might win them to the Lord. The hardest people to reach are the members of your own family. Even Jesus' family members didn't believe in Him until His resurrection. They thought He was crazy![53] And who was a better example than Jesus?

What if my parents tell me to do something that's a sin?

Like what? Making your bed? Taking the trash out? Doing your homework? If it was a clear cut issue—such as your parents telling you not to believe in Jesus—then you must obey God and not man. But that is rarely the case. The fact of the matter is, most parents have their children's best interests at heart. Most of us would not be here today if it were not for our parents' warnings and protection.

It's easy for kids to think their parents don't know what they're talking about. Just wait until the shoe is on the other foot, and you hear yourself saying things to your kids that your parents said to you (and you vowed you would never say). *We didn't have it so easy when I was a kid....Do you think I have a money tree somewhere?.... If your friends told you to jump off a cliff, would you do that, too?*

What great joy it brings to a parent when the lessons they have taught their children have been learned and followed. When the God of the parents also becomes the God of their children.

Let's look at the second of the commandments pertaining to our relationships with people.

commandment 6: you shall not murder

If ever there was a commandment that was ignored, it's this one. Nearly two million people a year become victims of violent crimes. Or contemplate the horrific act of mass murder on 9/11.

This commandment obviously forbids the taking of another human life for no justifiable reason. Without going in to a lot of depth in this brief fly-over, suffice it to say that the Bible does not condemn *all* killing. Numbers 35 plainly states the difference which God sets between killing and murder.

All murder, of course, is killing, but not all killing is murder. There are times when death is permissible, though not desirable. Self defense is one example. If someone were to break into your house with the intent of killing you or your family, Scripture allows you to defend yourself. Jesus told the disciples to take a sword with them on their travels. Why? Self defense!

When our military struck out at the wicked terrorists who attacked our nation, that is justifiable. It is not murder. (Murder is what *they* did.) It's self defense on a national scale.

We have all been aware of known killers condemned to death in different states across our country, and it is certainly biblical to do this.

Yes, you must execute anyone who murders another person, for to kill a person is to kill a living being made in God's image. (Genesis 9:6, NLT)

There is always a group of people who see it another way, holding vigil outside the prison where a murderer faces execution. They protest, they pray, and they usually hold up at least a few signs saying, "Thou shalt not kill."

Some would have a hard time understanding why we Bible-believing Christians would condone the execution of a murderer, and yet strongly oppose abortion. Yet you will find many who actually support abortion, and strongly oppose capital punishment. *That* to me is illogical, not the other position. They want to kill the innocent and spare the guilty. I want to spare the innocent and see justice brought to the guilty.

There are certainly good and sincere people on both sides of the issue of capital punishment. But there is something else to consider in this whole matter. In the Sermon on the Mount, Jesus takes the idea of murder one giant step further.

"You have heard that the law of Moses says, 'Do not murder. If you commit murder, you are subject to judgment.' But I say, if you are angry with someone, you are subject to judgment! If you call someone an idiot, you are in danger of being brought before the high council. And if you curse someone, you are in danger of the fires of hell." (Matthew 5:21-22, NLT)

Many people in the depths of their heart have anger and hatred to such a degree that they actually desire the death of another person. This is clearly forbidden in Scripture. In the book of First John, the apostle says, "Anyone who hates another Christian is really a murderer at heart. And you know that murderers don't have eternal life within them."[54]

The word used for *hate* in this passage means to habitually despise someone. It's not just a transient motion of the affections, but a deep rooted loathing.

Sometimes we will say, "I just hate her," "Or I can't stand him." God doesn't want His children to hate like that. Scripture tells us, "Get rid of all bitterness, rage and anger, brawling and slander, along with every form of malice. Be kind and compassionate to one another, forgiving each other, just as in Christ God forgave you."[55]

walking in the light

The Ten Commandments were given to *shut our mouths and open our eyes.* To drive us into the open arms of Jesus! Maybe you have had another god before Him. Perhaps you have taken His name in vain, dishonored your parents, or allowed yourself to hate someone.

James makes it clear that "whoever keeps the whole law and yet stumbles at just one point is guilty of breaking all of it."[56]

The Ten Commandments are a searing hot light that exposes reality. You might say, "I didn't realize what a sinner I was until reading these chapters."

Not long ago when I was driving, I came to an intersection and went straight through a red light. The truth is, I was daydreaming, and not paying attention to my driving. It wasn't intentional, but I still broke the law. And (wouldn't you know it?) right behind me was a cop. When those inevitable blue lights started flashing, I pulled over, and got out my driver's license and registration.

As soon as the officer walked up to the car, I told him, "I was wrong, I wasn't paying attention. It was crazy. I did that and it was my fault!" I was fully prepared to be ticketed. But the policeman said, "Most people don't admit it when they're wrong. Since you did, I'm going to let you go with a warning."

Listen, we all break the laws of God, intentionally and unintentionally. God wants us to come clean and admit failures and sin.

If we will turn to Jesus, He will forgive us of all our sin.

If we make it a habit to keep turning to Him at our first awareness of sin, we will "walk in the light, as He is in the light."

And that's a formula for a happy-happy life.

chapter ten

encounter at sinai, part 3: guarding your heart

commandment 7: you shall not commit adultery

A little boy who attended Sunday school one day where the Ten Commandments had been the topic. He came away a little confused about the meaning of the Seventh Commandment. After church he asked his father, "Daddy, what does it mean when it says, 'Thou shalt not commit agriculture'"?

There was hardly a beat between the question and the father's wise reply: "Son, that just means you're not supposed to plow the other man's field." The boy seemed satisfied with that response.

There is no need for us as Christians to have any doubt or confusion about God's prohibition against adultery. Simply stated, adultery is when you have sex with someone beside your spouse. Fornication is sex with someone you are not married to. According to the Bible, these are sins.

Sadly, every one of us knows at least one person, if not many more, who have fallen into this sin. If men and women across the world simply obeyed this one commandment, imagine what a different world it would be today. How many divorces would have been avoided? How many murders would disappear from the books? And emotional breakdowns? And suicides? How many families would be still together? How many fathers would still be at home to raise their children?

What an awesome destructive force is released by this sin! Lives beyond counting have been destroyed by it—or at the very least, rendered desperately unhappy.

Jesus once described his time as "a wicked and adulterous generation." If that was true then, how much more so now? Historians looking back at our time would have to say it was characterized by an obsession with things sexual. The sins of adultery and immorality are at the root of so many of our social ills today. You would think from watching and listening to our media today that adultery is now viewed as a recreational sport.

This year 10 million teenagers will engage in 126 million acts of sexual intercourse, resulting in 1 million pregnancies, 496,000 abortions, 134,000 miscarriages, and 490,000 births.

Maybe you've heard questions like these—or even asked them yourself: *"Why is it so wrong to have sex with someone anyway? So what if you're not married to them? As long as two consenting adults agree, what's the problem? Why has God laid down a law like this in the first place? Doesn't He know that young people have raging hormones? Why is God out to spoil all our fun? What's His problem anyway?"*

Know this: God gave us this law for our *good*.

Think about a couple of basic traffic laws. Stoplights, for instance. Don't you hate them? Whenever you have all the time in the world, you seem to hit green after green—for miles. But when you're in a rush…? You can't buy a green light!

Sometimes, it would be nice to just forget about them, wouldn't it?

Sure, but you'll pay the price.

You will eventually be injured or even die—and so will others.

Oh sure, you'll feel that initial rush when you sail through the red light in that first intersection while everyone else is waiting their turn. You might even make through two or three intersections. But it's only a matter of time. You're going to hit someone broadside, or they will smash into you…and the fun will be over.

Those traffic laws are there for your own good—not to make your life miserable. And you could say the same thing about the commandments of God. He gave them to us in His love.

Let's remember something very important: *God created sex.* Sometimes we may lose sight of that fact. Sexual intercourse is not evil. In fact, in it's proper, God-ordained, God-blessed context, it is very good. And that context is within a marriage relationship. Period!

> Give honor to marriage, and remain faithful to one another in marriage. God will surely judge people who are immoral and those who commit adultery. (Hebrews 13:4, NLT)

> Drink water from your own well—share your love only with your wife. (Proverbs 5:15, NLT)

Outside of its proper context, sex becomes unbelievably destructive—spiritually, emotionally, and even physically.

What is the real purpose of sex? Through the years, the Christian position on this issue has been mischaracterized as, "Sex is only for procreation, childbearing." But that's not what the Bible really says. While it is certainly the process through which procreation takes place, God also gave us sex as a way to create unity between a man and a woman. When a man and woman have sexual relations, a oneness takes place.

> Don't you realize that your bodies are actually parts of Christ? Should a man take his body, which belongs to Christ, and join it to a prostitute? Never! And don't you know that if a man joins himself to a prostitute, he becomes one body with her? For the Scriptures say, "The two are united into one." (1 Corinthians 6:15-17, NLT)

> Run away from sexual sin! No other sin so clearly affects the body as this one does. For sexual immorality is a sin against your own body . Or don't you know that your body is the temple of the Holy Spirit, who lives in you and was given to you by God? You do not belong to yourself, for God bought you with a high price. So you must honor God with your body. (1 Corinthians 6:18-20)

That is why there is no such thing as a quick, one night fling that doesn't mean anything.

It means plenty.

Sex is not some casual toy. It is a gift from God to be saved for that person with whom you want to become one.

"But wait," some might protest. "This doesn't hurt anyone." Doesn't it? *It hurts you!*

A University of Tennessee study among young women found that "There seems to be a direct correlation between illicit sexual behavior and serious emotional problems."

Sex outside of wedlock can hurt the future marriage. The University of Oregon did a study among young men, and found that those who engage in premarital sexual relationships make poor marital risks.

It doesn't hurt anyone? What about the teen pregnancies? Each year more than 1 million teens become pregnant. Many of these babies never make it to term. One out of every five abortions is performed on a woman under age 20, and 4 out of every 10 teenage pregnancies ends in abortion. In other words, about 400,000 of the 1.6 million abortions occurring annually are performed on teenage mothers.

You don't think *that* is hurting someone? What about the innocent baby being killed? What about that young mother who (no matter what pro-abortion propaganda claims) will carry that guilt for years to come?

Free sex doesn't hurt anyone? What about AIDS? Did you know that AIDS is the leading killer of Americans between the ages of 25 and 44? Twenty-five percent of all HIV infections are found in people under the age of 22. The rate of infection from sexually transmitted diseases: syphilis, herpes, gonorrhea, and AIDS has reached epidemic proportions.

How do we deal with this? We are told to have "safe sex." The federal government has spent almost 3 billion of our taxes since 1970 to promote contraceptives and safe sex among our teenagers. Condoms, however, have a failure rate ranging from 15 to 36 percent!

Think of it like this. Imagine you find yourself on a flight where the captain announces, "Ladies and gentlemen, we are having some mechanical difficulties. The mechanics tell us there is a 15 percent chance we will not make it to our destination, but not to worry. After all, this is a safe flight!" Would you stay on board or head for the door? Or what if he said, there was a 36 percent chance the plane wouldn't make it?

Does that sound safe or sane to you?

I have a better idea than safe sex. *Save sex.* God has told us not to involve ourselves in illicit sexual relationships for very good reason! That is why this pervasive and powerful sin made the top 10.

> Listen to me, my sons, and pay attention to my words. Don't let your hearts stray away toward her. Don't wander down her wayward path. For she has been the ruin of many; numerous men have been her victims. Her house is the road to the grave. Her bedroom is the den of death. (Proverbs 7:24-27, NLT)

The passages concerning this sin are every bit as clear in the New Testament as those of the Old.

> Do you not know that the wicked will not inherit the kingdom of God? Do not be deceived: Neither the sexually immoral nor idolaters nor adulterers nor male prostitutes nor homosexual offenders nor thieves nor the greedy nor drunkards nor slanderers nor swindlers will inherit the kingdom of God. (1 Corinthians 6:9-10, NIV)

> Marriage is honorable among all, and the bed undefiled; but fornicators and adulterers God will judge. (Hebrews 13:4)

> God wants you to be holy, so you should keep clear of all sexual sin. Then each of you will control your body and live in holiness and honor. (1 Thessalonians 4:3-4, NLT)

You might say, "I've never committed this sin." That's great, but remember how Jesus said if you hated someone, it was the same as killing him? He also said something similar about the sin of adultery.

> "You have heard that the law of Moses says, 'Do not commit adultery.' But I say, anyone who even looks at a woman with lust in his eye has already committed adultery with her in his heart. So if your eye—even if it is your good eye—causes you to lust, gouge it out and throw it away. It is better for you to lose one part of your body than for your whole body to be thrown into hell. And if your hand—even if it is your stronger hand—causes you to sin, cut it off and throw it away. It is better for you to lose one part of your body than for your whole body to be thrown into hell." (Matthew 5:27-30)

"Looks at a woman." Obviously, Jesus doesn't mean a casual glance here, or all the men in the world would have to go around with blinders on. In the Greek, this term refers to the *continuous* act of looking. In this usage, the idea isn't that of an incidental or involuntary glance, but of intentional and repeated gazing.

Jesus isn't speaking here of unexpected and unavoidable exposure to sexual temptation. It's almost everywhere! It is the person who intentionally puts himself in the place of vulnerability, or if he is exposed, gives the Devil a foothold by allowing it into his thought processes. This is why Job said, "I made a covenant with my eyes not to look lustfully at a girl" (Job 31:1, NIV).

Some would say you just can't resist it. It's impossible for a man or a woman with a sex drive in this day and age not to fall.

That's simply not true. It takes more of a ramp-up to commit adultery than you might think. What we must recognize is that this aspect of human nature is combustible, and no one is immune to the flames. Keep your hand near enough to the fire, and hold it there long enough, and it *will* burn.

> But each one is tempted when he is drawn away by his own desires and enticed. Then, when desire has conceived,

it gives birth to sin; and sin, when it is full-grown, brings forth death. (James 1:14-15)

One time I came upon my young son Jonathan playing video games before school started—and he knew very well he was breaking the rules. With a guilty look on his face he said, "I couldn't resist myself."

That's not a bad way to define temptation. When we get tempted and give in to it, we like to place the blame on someone or something else.

The Devil made me do it.

That person enticed me—trapped me.

I'm not responsible.

You remember the story of David and his fall with Bathsheba. David wasn't at fault for happening to see Bathsheba bathing. One wonders if Bathsheba knew he would be there, and intentionally put herself in a place where she would be seen. Remember this is a two way street! If lustful looking is bad, then those who dress and expose themselves with the desire to be looked at and lusted after are not less guilty—and perhaps more so!

Girls, ladies…think about what you are wearing (or not wearing) before you leave your house. How would you feel if it was Jesus who would be taking you out somewhere? That doesn't mean you can't wear stylish clothing. But don't dress in such a way as to encourage a guy to lust after you. And you know what that means better than I do.

"But Greg, you might protest, some guys would lust after a *tree!*" True. But that doesn't excuse you from having some modesty! David's sin was a continuous look, and then taking dramatic action as he misused his considerable power as king and had her brought to his bedroom.

What we must do to the best of our abilities is to *guard our minds.* If you're sitting in a theater or watching a movie at someone's house with some friends and a scene comes up that offends you, get up and walk out. If something sexually suggestive pops up on TV (seemingly once every two minutes or so), turn the

channel or turn it off. Be careful where you go surfing on the
net. Chat rooms, too. If a conversation with a member of the
opposite sex becomes sexually suggestive, terminate it.

Check out something before you watch it, read it, or listen
to it. Simply telling yourself, "I can handle it," could be nothing
more than self deception.

Scripture urges us to bring "every thought into captivity
to the obedience of Christ" (2 Corinthians 10:4-5).

How seriously did Jesus treat this temptation to lust?
As you will see in the following passage, He doesn't recommend
kid gloves.

> So if your hand or foot causes you to sin, cut it off and
> throw it away. It is better to enter heaven crippled or lame
> than to be thrown into the unquenchable fire with both
> of your hands and feet. And if your eye causes you to sin,
> gouge it out and throw it away. It is better to enter heaven
> half blind than to have two eyes and be thrown into hell.
> (Matthew 18:8-9, NLT)

With these strong words, Jesus points out the way of deliverance from this sin. Obviously, He's not speaking literally. If the
problem is in the heart, what good is gouging out an eye or cut-
ting off a hand? If the right eye were gone the left one could still
look lustfully. If the right hand were cut off, the left one could
still carry on sinful acts.

In the Jewish culture, "the right hand" represented a person's
best skills and most precious faculties. The right eye represented
one's best vision, and the right hand one's best skills.

Here's our Lord's point: *We should be willing to take strong
action—to give up whatever is necessary—to keep us from
falling into sin.* Anything that morally or spiritually traps us,
that causes us to fall into sin or stay in sin, should be eliminated
quickly and totally.

commandment 8: you shall not steal

Stealing runs rampant in today's culture, becoming far more commonplace than we may realize. We live in such a thieving culture we don't even notice how bad it is. We've become accustomed to it.

But think about it. Many of us think of alarm systems as standard options on a new car. Clerks at many gas stations and convenience stores take our money from behind bulletproof glass. Signs tell us that cashiers can't open safes. Tiny red lights blink on our car doors and dashboards indicating the alarm system is on. We place little signs in prominent positions on our front lawns, warning of a home alarm system.

Even the look of the one hundred dollar bill has changed. To thwart high-tech counterfeiters, the Treasury Department began phasing in a new design earlier this year, the first change since 1921. Why? Because people steal everywhere!

Consider these statistics: Although 1 in 5 homes have burglar alarms, 16 million homes were burglarized last year, with losses totaling up to 19.1 billion dollars. Bandits robbed people in the streets 20 million times last year. There is a robbery in our nation every 48 seconds Two million cars are stolen every year. In New York City, theft has become so common that the police won't even take a report.

A *Newsweek* article titled *The Thrill of Theft*, states: "Each year, ordinary people shoplift $13 billion of lipsticks, batteries and bikinis from stores. …Retailers like Brandy Samson, who manages a jewelry and accessories store in the Sherman Oaks, California Fashion Square, uses shoplifting as a guide to taste. "We know what's hot among teens by seeing what they steal," she says.[57]

In a recent article in *USA Today*, the reporter states that nearly half of U.S. workers admit to taking unethical or illegal actions in the past year. Those include one or more from a list of 25 actions, including cheating on an expense account, paying or accepting kickbacks, secretly forging signatures, and trading sex for sales. Workers say it's getting worse, with 57 percent saying they feel more pressure toward unethical behavior than 5 years ago, and 40 percent say it's gotten worse over the last year.

And check this out! Retail stores lose more to employee theft than to shoplifting, according to a University of Florida survey. Most employee theft goes unreported, but employee screening company guards mark estimates at $120 billion a year. Even though most instinctively know that stealing is wrong, many couldn't tell you *why*.

In a recent study by Ohio State University, researchers learned that 90 percent of teens agreed that stealing was wrong, yet 37 percent of high schoolers say they have stolen from a store in the last 12 months. Those who had not stolen anything in that time period were asked why. The number one reason? "I might get caught." The number two reason: The other person might try to get even. The number three reason? I might not need the item.

Newsflash! *How about because God says "You shall not steal?"* Here are some actual excuses used by people who were caught stealing.

"I was going to come back and pay for it."

"I got cheated at this store last week and I'm only evening the score." "It was just a prank."

"You mean this isn't a free sample?"

I read about a man named Natron Fubble who tried to rob a Miami deli, but the owner broke Fubble's nose by hitting him with a giant salami. Fubble fled and hid in the trunk of a parked car. The car, however, belonged to an undercover police team that happened to be trailing a different criminal. After five days, the officers heard Fubble whimpering in the trunk and arrested him.

In Belmont, New Hampshire a teenager robbed a local convenience store. Getting away with a pocket full of change, the boy walked home. What he didn't realize, however, was that he had holes in both of his front pockets! A trail of quarters and dimes led police directly to his house.

Police in Wichita, Kansas, arrested a 22 year old man at an airport hotel after he tried to pass 2 (counterfeit) $16 bills!

When two service stations attendants in Ionia, Michigan refused to hand over the cash to an intoxicated robber, the man threatened to call the police. They still refused, so the robber called the police and was arrested.

But it's not just people robbing stores or holding up service stations. The temptations to steal are constant: When you receive too much change at the store and keep it. When you take those office supplies home for personal use. When you take that help from the government you don't need.

Stealing has become epidemic in our society. We're shocked today when someone actually returns a lost wallet. (Unless the honest individual happens to be a Christian.)

I received a letter from a man who lost his wallet at one of our services. There was $1,700 cash in it. A young man brought it to his home and asked nothing in return. He wrote me, wanting to track him down to give him a reward.

Here is what God says about stealing: "Let him who stole steal no longer, but rather let him labor, working with his hands what is good, that he may have something to give him who has need" (Ephesians 4:28).

I see three principles in this verse.

1. steal no longer.

Don't ever take anything that belongs to another individual, business—or whomever. Don't try to justify it in your mind because of "extenuating circumstances." It's wrong before God, and His eyes miss nothing! Scripture says, "God is closely watching you, and he weighs carefully everything you do" (Proverbs 5:21, TLB).

If you have taken something, if at all possible, *give it back*.

Remember the story of Zacchaeus? He had made his living taking advantage of others, overcharging them in their taxes. But one day Jesus saw him up in that tree and invited Himself over for a meal. The two disappeared behind Zacchaeus's closed door.

When they reemerged, Zacchaeus stood up and said: "Look, Lord! Here and now I give half of my possessions to the poor, and if I have cheated anybody out of anything, I will pay back four times the amount."[58]

2. do something useful.

Renew your commitment to work for everything you have. Like it or not, man is to earn his bread by the sweat of his brow. Paul minced no words on this point:

> For even when we were with you, we commanded you this: If anyone will not work, neither shall he eat. (2 Thessalonians 3:10)

Earn your own living. The world doesn't owe you one, and your parents can't support you for the rest of your life. Get a job, and learn a work ethic!

> And whatever you do, do it heartily, as to the Lord and not to men. (Colossians 3:23)

3. share what you have.

Sharing is the opposite of stealing. God wants us to help others who are in need, and we need to be gainfully employed to have resources to do that.

I'll tell you one another person we steal from...*God*.

> "Will a man rob God?
> Yet you have robbed Me!
> But you say,
> 'In what way have we robbed You?'
> In tithes and offerings."
> (Malachi 3:8)

The Bible teaches that each Christian should give to God on a regular basis. "Well," you might say, "I *would* give, but I just don't have any money left over for God." That's why the first check you write every pay period needs to go to the Lord, trusting Him to meet all your other needs. Our obedience and faithfulness in this matter is a pretty accurate barometer of our relationship with the Lord.

This brings us to the Ninth Commandment.

commandment 9:
do not bear false witness

Strictly speaking, this commandment was originally focused against perjuring oneself in a judicial trial. Yet it certainly applies to lying in all its forms.

To know what a lie is, I must first understand what truth is. George Barna conducted a poll and asked adults if they agreed with the following statement: *There are no absolute standards for morals and ethics.* Seven out of ten said they agreed with it! With this kind of outlook, it's easy to see why lying and deception are so much a part of our culture.

Another survey reported that 65 percent of high schoolers admitted to cheating on an exam within the previous 12 month period. On the college level, 24 percent of college students said they would lie to get or keep a job, and 47 percent of adults would accept an auto body repairman's offer to include unrelated damages in insurance claim. The book, *The Day America Told The Truth*,[59] pointed out the following:

> Americans lie. They lie more than we had ever thought possible before the study. But they told us the truth about how much they lie. Just about everyone lies! 91% of us lie regularly. The majority of us find it hard to get through a week without lying. 1 in 5 can't make it through a single day without lying. And we're talking about conscious, premeditated lies. When we refrain from lying, it's less often because we think it is wrong (only 45%), than for a variety of other reasons, among them the fear of being caught (17%). We lie to just about everyone, and the better we know someone the likelier we are to have told them a serious lie.[60]

The Bible has a lot to say about this. In Proverbs 6, God speaks of the seven things He hates.

> These six things the LORD hates,
> Yes, seven are an abomination to Him:
> A proud look,
> A lying tongue,
> Hands that shed innocent blood,
> A heart that devises wicked plans,
> Feet that are swift in running to evil,
> A false witness who speaks lies,
> And one who sows discord among brethren.
> (Proverbs 6:16-19)

Hates in the passage above means to "hate personally a personal enemy." I certainly wouldn't want to be doing something God specifically says He hates, would you? It's worth noting that two of the seven things God hates refer to dishonesty.

Why does God speak so strongly about lying? Because it's so *destructive*.

> Like a club or a sword or a sharp arrow is the man who gives false testimony against his neighbor.
> (Proverbs 25:18)

The Living Bible renders the passage like this: "Telling lies about someone is as harmful as hitting him with an axe, or wounding him with a sword, or shooting him with a sharp arrow."

From passages like these, we could safely conclude that God hates lying in any form. He hates it because He is the source of truth. In fact, He used that very word to describe His character. Jesus said, "I am the truth."

Scripture tells us that it is impossible for God to lie.[61] In dramatic contrast, Jesus calls Satan "the father of lies" (John 8:44). When we lie, we are behaving more like children of the Devil than children of God.

Have you been telling lies about others lately? God says of the liar, "He who works deceit shall not dwell within My house;

he who tells lies shall not continue in My presence" (Psalm 101:7). This means that if you are telling lies (and there really are no "little white ones"), you are in sin against God.

Paul writes, "Do not lie to each other, since you have taken off your old self with its practices and have put on the new self, which is being renewed in knowledge in the image of its Creator" (Colossians 3:9, NIV).

We know it's wrong…so why do we do it? Often because we have been caught doing something wrong. The classic example of "whoppers of all time" was Aaron with the golden calf.

> [Moses] turned to Aaron. "What did the people do to you?" he demanded. "How did they ever make you bring such terrible sin upon them?"
>
> "Don't get upset, sir," Aaron replied. "You yourself know these people and what a wicked bunch they are. They said to me, 'Make us some gods to lead us, for something has happened to this man Moses, who led us out of Egypt.' So I told them, 'Bring me your gold earrings.' When they brought them to me, I threw them into the fire—and out came this calf!" (Exodus 32:21-24, NLT)

Isn't that amazing? You happen to throw a bunch of earrings into the pot, and out leaps a golden calf!

A survey on lying in the *Washington Post* magazine cited the two principle reasons people tell falsehoods are to save face, and to keep from offending someone else.

We've all been faced with those situations when telling the truth is uncomfortable, to say the least.

A wife asks her husband, "Honey, do I look *fat* in this?"

The wisest answer here is an incomplete one. "Wow, I think you look great tonight." You don't have to go into detail!

Or you've just choked down a horrible meal as a guest in someone's home, and they ask, "How was it?"

"Umm…" you say, "I've never eaten anything like that in my life!"

Or someone sings a solo and just butchers the song. They come up to you afterward and say, "How'd I do?" What do you say? Well, you try not to state the obvious, while not telling an outright lie.

"It was one of the most fascinating performances I have ever heard. Your voice was distinct and stood out from all the rest."

An outright lie, however, is an outright lie. And the "little" ones can easily lead to more serious ones.

You say, "I'm not home," when you really are.

Or, "I forgot," when you really didn't.

Or, "It's good to see you!" when you don't feel that way at all.

Or, "I love your outfit," when you really hate it.

Or, "I was just getting ready to call you," when you had no intention. Or, "I'll be praying for you," when you know you probably won't.

So you say you never lie? Maybe you lie more than you realize! Deception wears a number of different guises.

1. gossip

There's another manifestation of bearing false witness that often tries to cover itself with a cloak of respectability. But it's poison through and through.

Gossip.

It topples governments, wrecks marriages, splits churches, ruins careers, destroys reputations, causes nightmare, spawns suspicion, and generates grief. Even its name hisses. *Gossssssip.*

> A gossip betrays a confidence;
> so avoid a man who talks too much.
> (Proverbs 20:19, NIV)

Within my circle of friends, there are certain people whom I know can keep a confidence. And then there are others…. If I tell them, "Don't tell anyone," it will be on CNN that night!

Gossip often veils itself in "acceptable ways," such as….
"Have you heard?"
"Did you know?"
"I don't believe it's true, but I heard that…."
"I probably shouldn't tell you this, but I know you'll pray…."
There's nothing wrong with conveying accurate information in appropriate situations. But the question is, are you *sure* that what you're about to say is true? Have you checked your facts? Have you gone to the person you're intending to talk about?

There's a little acrostic I came across that's helped a lot of people think twice about talking behind someone's back. In fact, it's the word T.H.I.N.K.

(T) Is it True? (H) Will it Help? (I) Is it Inspiring? (N) Is it Necessary? (K) Is it Kind?

"But Greg," you say, "if I applied those standards, 90 percent of what I say should never be said!" So be it. Maybe you're like the guy who told his friend, "I will never repeat gossip…so please listen carefully the first time!"

2. flattery

This is one of the most subtle forms of deceit. One definition of flattery is saying things to a certain person's face that you would never say behind his or her back.

It's tempting to flatter someone to get something from them—so you tell them something you think they want to hear. You tell them they are better than they really are, saying things to them you don't actually believe yourself. It is a form of lying, and as with all lies, can be very damaging.

3. exaggeration

Would it be an exaggeration to say we all do this?

We talk about that Alaskan King salmon that got away ("It must have been fifty pounds…"), or we tell someone "You've been on my mind all day" (would you believe ten minutes?).

We may exaggerate our skills to get a promotion. Or just stretch the facts to make the story we're telling more interesting or juicy. Harmless, you say? Not really. In the first place, it begins to erode your credibility, causing people to doubt your character. And more significantly, any form of lying opens the door to the Father of Lies…and that's a door you want to keep firmly closed.

4. keeping silence.

How could saying nothing be a lie? This could be on those occasions when we hear somebody say something we know for a fact is not true, and we remain silent. Someone may be slamming a friend or an acquaintance, and you know what they are saying is off base. But you don't say a word; you let the destructive words stand. This is slander by silence, complicity by passivity. And it is as deceitful as if you had said it yourself.

And now we come to the final commandment in God's top ten. While the previous commandments we've discussed focus mostly on externals, this one has to do with our heart. The other commandments focus on actions, while this one deals with a state of mind.

commandment 10: you shall not covet

This Tenth Command reminds us that God cares about what goes on between our ears. We're kidding ourselves if we think God only takes note of external behavior.

> "You shall not covet your neighbor's house; you shall not covet your neighbor's wife, nor his male servant, nor his female servant, nor his ox, nor his donkey, nor anything that is your neighbor's." (Exodus 20:17-18)

Coveting isn't simply desiring something you don't have. *It is to be devoured by desire for something that is not yours.* The New Testament Greek translation of the Hebrew word for "covet" means to lust, to pant after something. It means to set the heart or to eagerly desire that which belongs to another.

A Roman Catholic priest, who had heard the confessions of some 2,000 persons, said he had heard men confess iniquities of every kind—including adultery and even murder—but he had never heard any man confess to committing the sin of covetousness.

How does coveting work? It begins with the eyes. The eyes look at an object, the mind admires it, the will goes over to it, and the body moves in to possess it.

Let's not misunderstand: You may admire your friend's car—and even buy one like it—but that is not coveting. Copying, maybe, but not coveting. Now if you were to find his car in a parking lot, jimmy the lock, hot wire the car, and drive away with it, that's coveting—and stealing, too. If you look at it, admire it, and your will desires it, the your body moves over to possess it, you have violated the Tenth Commandment. That is coveting which has led to action. In this case, to grand theft auto!

It's not wrong to desire a wife, either, but to desire the wife of another man is coveting. Coveting is a powerful and often underestimated sin. It can cripple you spiritually and ultimately destroy you. It must not be simply shrugged off or left unchecked.

Paul wrote this strong warning to Timothy: "For the love of money is a root of all kinds of evil, for which some have strayed from the faith in their greediness, and pierced themselves through with many sorrows" (1 Timothy 6:10). Judas betrayed the Savior of the world for thirty pieces of silver—that he never enjoyed for a moment!

It's not a sin to want to be successful in business, and make a good living. But when you become obsessed with it, when you are willing to do whatever it takes to get there, when it becomes the most important thing in life to you, coveting has become idolatry.

> Therefore put to death your members which are on the earth: fornication, uncleanness, passion, evil desire, and covetousness, which is idolatry. (Colossians 3:5-6)

The story of King David's great sin in 2 Samuel 12 is a classic case of a man who started with coveting—and slid straight down from there into sins that were far worse. *He coveted another man's wife...he stole her...he committed adultery...he was an accomplice to murder...he tried to cover it up.*

Have you ever stolen, lied, or coveted? Of course you have. We've all broken God's Ten Commandments. And we all would be without hope and without God in the world if He had not provided a remedy for our sins, a way back into intimacy and fellowship with Him.

You need to repent, change your direction, and ask God to forgive you right now.

Sometimes reading things like this can be a bit uncomfortable. We know very well we have violated some of these commands, and we don't like to have it pointed out to us—even in private. It's like going to the dentist with a killer toothache, and he tells you he needs to drill, and maybe do a root canal. You initially feel like getting out of that chair and walking out the door. But if you want to stop the pain and not have it get even worse, you must do it.

In the same way, God convicts us of our sin not to drive us to despair, but rather to send us into the open arms of Jesus. He knows what you've done. He has already paid for it at Calvary's cross.

He says "Come unto me...."

There isn't a single sin or broken command beyond His forgiving, restoring, healing power.

That's why we call Him the Savior.

chapter eleven

encounter at the summit: experiencing his glory

We've all walked our way through the different stages of friendship.

When you first meet someone, you're very polite. You actually listen when they speak, give eye contact, and even laugh at their lame jokes.

But once you become real friends the formalities begin to fade, and the real business of friendship begins. You're more honest. You feel more freedom to speak your mind, to show your emotions. In fact, you let your guard down, and take the risk of letting your friend see what's going on inside your heart.

This progression might be symbolized by free access into your friend's kitchen. If he or she takes you there, that in itself is a mark of progress. Why? Because if you really don't want someone to stay very long, you usher your guest into your front room.

If you're new friends, you might be hanging out in your buddy's kitchen and see something good to eat—like a nice, ripe peach—on the counter. But since you still don't know each other all that well, you don't ask for the peach...you wait for it to offered. (Maybe stare at it for a minute or two, so they get the idea!) But if you've known that individual for a long time, you might just pick up that peach and bite into it without asking. Why? Because your friend has invited you to make yourself at home—and means it.

Obviously, there are stages of intimacy and understanding in marriage, as well. Do you remember when you first met your spouse-to-be? Remember working so hard to make the best possible impression? You wanted to put your best foot forward, and always say "the right thing." I remember having a big crush on a girl in high school, and was so anxious about calling her that I made up a written list of things to talk about in advance. A script!

Finally, you popped the big question to the love of your life (I kind of slipped it in). During engagement you got to know each other even better. And finally your wedding day arrived.

When you've been married for awhile, you can actually begin to anticipate what your spouse wants—what he or she might be thinking. You can walk into a room and feel the vibes, knowing immediately whether your mate is in a good or bad mood. Sometimes in conversation, you even finish each other's sentences.

Most husbands—at least the wise ones—have figured out that women don't always say what they really mean. You need to learn to interpret. And because you love your wife, you're willing to take the time to do that...to find out what she's really thinking and how she's really feeling. It might take you awhile to draw it out, but if you are lovingly persistent, you'll come to an understanding.

But women need interpretation skills, too. Let me give you a few "for instances."

- When a man says to a woman, "It's a guy thing," what he really means is: There is no rational thought pattern connected with this, and you have no chance at all of making it logical.

- When a man says to a woman, "Can I help with dinner?" what he really means is: Why isn't it already on the table?

- When he says, "Uh-huh...sure, honey," or "Yes, dear," what he really means is: Absolutely nothing! It's a conditioned response.

- When he says, "It would take too long to explain," what he really means is: I have no idea how it works.

- When he says, "Take a break, honey. You're working too hard," what he actually means is: I can't hear the game over the vacuum cleaner.

- When he says, "That's interesting, dear," what he really means is: Are you still talking?

- When he says, "You know how bad my memory is," what he really means is: I can remember the theme song to "F-Troop," the address of the first girl I ever kissed, and the vehicle identification numbers of every car I've ever owned—but I forgot your birthday!

- When he says, "I can't find it," what he means is: It didn't fall into my outstretched hand, so I'm completely clueless.

- When he says, "You look terrific!" what he really means is: Oh please don't try on one more outfit, I'm starving!

- When he says, "I'm not lost! I know exactly where we are," what he really means is: No one will ever see us alive again!

In this chapter, we'll encounter the story of a man in the book of Exodus who truly knew the Lord personally—not only as God, but as a close friend. And there was no communication breakdown here.

"a great sin"

Moses was on intimate terms with the Lord of the universe, and could freely speak his mind. Scripture says that "the LORD spoke to Moses face to face, as a man speaks to his friend" (Exodus 33:11).The Lord revealed things to him He had never revealed to a human being before.

Then one day, deep in prayer, Moses asked the unthinkable—a request almost without parallel in human history to this point.

Moses asked to actually see God.

Shocking? Yes. But friends can ask special favors of friends. And God wasn't offended! In fact, He had been in the process of drawing Moses out, showing him what prayer was really all about.

In the last few chapters, we considered the Ten Commandments, given by God. They were personally delivered from the

Lord to His friend Moses, up on Mount Sinai. Aaron had been left in charge of the people in his brother's absence. But instead of waiting with baited breath for the Word of the Lord, the Israelites had turned to full-tilt idolatry and gross immorality.

After seeing this debacle for himself, Moses told the people, "You have committed a great sin."[62] This raises an interesting question: Are some sins greater or worse than others? Some might say, "No, sin is sin. It's all the same." But that's not totally true. According to Scripture, there are some sins that truly are worse than others.

Now, in a broad sense, all sin—from the smallest infraction to the most grievous crime—separates us from God. Jesus made this clear in the Sermon on the Mount, when He pointed out that lusting was a sin as well as committing adultery, and hating was a sin as well as murder.

They won't send you to jail for hating someone, but count on it, you'll go to prison for murder—and maybe to death row. And though it's wrong and sinful to coddle lust in your heart, it doesn't have the same life-blasting ramifications of adultery.

Jesus drew a distinction between sins when He was speaking to Pontius Pilate. He told the Roman governor, "You could have no power at all against Me unless it had been given you from above. Therefore the one who delivered Me to you has the greater sin."[63]

Jesus was either referring to Caiaphas, the High Priest, or to Judas, the betrayer. Both of these men knew very well Jesus was innocent, and that what they were doing was dead wrong. When we have been schooled in the Scripture as Caiaphas had been schooled or exposed to the truth and power of God like Judas, we are essentially without excuse.

This leads to the "unforgivable sin," which is blasphemy against the Holy Spirit. The work of the Holy Spirit is to show us our need for Jesus, our need for a Savior. To "blaspheme"

Him means to reject or disregard Him—in essence, to "blow Him off." It is to say, "I know the gospel is true, but I refuse to accept it or to follow Jesus."

This is the greatest sin of all.

Israel had committed a great sin in the shadow of Mount Sinai. Why was it a "great" sin? Because, like Caiaphas, they *knew* better. They were God's chosen, covenant people. They had seen His fearsome power demonstrated on their behalf.

Who could forget…

…the ten devastating plagues that shook the nation of Egypt to the core?

…that wild wind that split the Red Sea down the middle, making an escape route for Israel, and creating a watery grave for the pursuing Egyptians?

…the manna sent from heaven to sustain millions of people cut off from provision in the wilderness?

And on top of all that, the people of Israel had solemnly promised to obey the Lord on three separate occasions. In Exodus 19, for instance, there was this exchange:

Moses returned from the mountain and called together the leaders of the people and told them what the LORD had said. They all responded together, "We will certainly do everything the LORD asks of us." So Moses brought the people's answer back to the LORD. (vv. 7-8, NLT)

Jesus said, "From everyone who has been given much, much will be demanded; and from the one who has been entrusted with much, much more will be asked."[64]

Not only are some sins worse than others, but *all* sin must be dealt with. And Moses was about to deal with the shocking sin in the camp of Israel.

We already know of the guilt of the people worshiping a golden calf combined with an unbridled sexual orgy. But what made it all so much worse was the utter failure of Israel's leadership in the whole affair. While Moses was up on the mountain meeting with the Lord, Aaron, Hur, and the Levites had full authority to quell this uprising—and should have! Aaron heard the people clamoring for an idol. But instead of stopping this surge of popular sentiment cold, he figured he would make the best of it. He tried to justify it before God by throwing a burnt offering into the equation and calling it "a feast to the LORD."[65]

This lame attempt at "compromise," however, only outraged the Lord even more, and He came within a hair's breadth of wiping out the whole nation (or so it seemed), sparing Moses alone.

Moses was angry, too, but he interceded for his rebellious people, and God turned away from His wrath.

This is why I have a problem with a ministry philosophy that centers around "meeting people's felt needs." Here was a nation that had no idea what they really needed. Their "felt need" was for an idol. But what they really needed was faith in the God who had brought them this far.

truth and consequences

Though God pardoned Israel, there was still a price to be paid for their sin. This reminds us that God *in His grace* forgives our sins, but God *in His government* allows sin to work out its consequences in human life.

For instance, God forgave David for his sin of adultery with Bathsheba. But He also warned David that "the sword shall never depart from your house...."[66] And it didn't. To his lasting grief, David saw his own behavior repeated in the lives of his children.

Sin will have its pound of flesh. It will cost, and cost *big*. When Paul wrote that "the wages of sin is death," he meant more than physical death and the grave. It is also a principle of death that casts a shadow over life itself—over every worthwhile thing in our lives, robbing us of joy, peace, and contentment.

Moses came down from the crown of Mount Sinai and saw the people completely given over to idolatry and immorality.

And when he confronted Aaron—the High Priest!—he got one of the lamest excuses anyone has ever scraped together.

Angry to the core, Moses gave the people an ultimatum. He cried out, "'Whoever is on the LORD's side—come to me!' And all the sons of Levi gathered themselves together to him" (Exodus 32:26). Moses commanded these loyal Levites to slay the offenders without pity, and 3,000 people were slain that day.

removing the cancer

Some will say, "That's not fair! How could a God of love do something like that?"

We only show our ignorance when we make statements like that. Here's a newsflash. God doesn't owe you an explanation as to why He does or doesn't do certain things. He doesn't even owe you the time of day! And even if He did give us His reasons, we can't assume we would even begin to understand them. A finite human mind trying to grapple with the thoughts of God would be like wiring the full power of Bonneville Dam to a five-watt flashlight bulb. We couldn't handle them for an instant.

> "For as the heavens are higher than the earth,
> So are My ways higher than your ways,
> And My thoughts than your thoughts."
> (Isaiah 55:9)

> Oh, what a wonderful God we have! How great are his riches and wisdom and knowledge! How impossible it is for us to understand his decisions and his methods! For who can know what the Lord is thinking? Who knows enough to be his counselor? (Romans 11:33-34, NLT)

One thing we can be very sure of is that God hates sin, and it cannot be tolerated. It must be dealt with swiftly, lest it spread and do even more harm. The Bible compares it to leaven, something that grows quickly. It is like a cancer that left untreated will metastasize, spread, and kill.

It's hard for us to fathom a God of righteousness and judgment in this day of unconditional "tolerance" and political correctness. Some would even try to differentiate between the "God of wrath" in the Old Testament, and the "God of love" in the New. As if He had somehow evolved and changed, seeing things from a different point of view.

Not so! He is the same God, who is just and loving in both testaments of the Bible. He declares, "For I am the LORD, I do not change" (Malachi 3:6).

And believe me, you wouldn't want it any other way.

Some might say *"I don't believe in a God of judgment, just a God of love."* That may be true, but the God you are choosing to worship *is not real.* The French philosopher Voltaire once wrote, "God made man in His image, and man returned the favor."

Have you heard of "The Temple of the Thousand Buddhas."? It's an unusual place of worship in Kyoto, Japan, where worshipers can literally design their own deities. The temple is filled with more than a thousand likenesses of Buddha, each one a little different from the next, allowing worshipers to pick and choose which they like best. Devotees of Buddha often try to find the likeness they feel most resembles themselves.

And that's exactly what we do when we say, "Well, *my* God would never do thus and so…." Or maybe, "I agree with this part of what the Bible says, but not that *part.*"

What you are doing, whether you intend to or not, is remaking God in your own image, and that is idolatry. It's no different from Aaron forming a golden calf and declaring, "This is your god, O Israel, that brought you out of the land of Egypt!"

standing in the gap

The Lord told Moses He was fed up with the Israelites: "I have seen this people, and indeed it is a stiff-necked people! Now therefore, let Me alone, that My wrath may burn hot against them and I may consume them. And I will make of you a great nation" (Exodus 32:9-10).

God was testing Moses. I don't believe it was His intention to annihilate the whole nation, but to see if Moses would pray, intercede, and stand in the gap for the Israelites.

It's the same today. God is still looking for intercessors… people who are willing to stand in the gap.

The gospel of John tells the story of a desperate father whose son was at death's door. Though part of a royal family, this man found Jesus and humbled himself before Him—imploring and begging Him to touch his dear son.

Jesus' response was a little unusual—maybe not what you'd expect: "Unless you people see signs and wonders, you will by no means believe."[67]

As with Moses, Jesus was testing this distraught father. In reality, Jesus was not directing these words of rebuke to the man, but to the fickle crowd standing around observing these things.

That father patiently waited. Not to be deterred, he again petitioned Jesus. "Sir, come to my house before my child dies."

This man had passed the test, and stood strong as both a godly father and a true intercessor. And Jesus replied, "Go your way, your son lives."

Many times we pray and don't see the results we so desperately want. This is especially true as we pray for our children. But the story of that father, and the one of Moses crying out to God for his people, teaches us this important principle: When praying for the salvation of a soul, the intervention of God in a life, *don't give up!* You are praying according to the will of God. You can know that for sure, because Scripture says, "God is not willing that any should perish but that all should come to repentance" (2 Peter 3:9).

This is not unlike what the Lord said to Abraham when He told him, "Take now your son, your only son Isaac, whom you love, and go to the land of Moriah, and offer him there as a burnt offering on one of the mountains of which I shall tell you"

(Genesis 22:2). It was never God's intention to take Isaac's life (God has never sanctioned human sacrifice), but rather to test and mature His servant Abraham.

Abraham passed his test with flying colors, and so did Moses. In fact, Moses offered himself in the place of his people—even willing to give up his hope of heaven if God would spare them.

Moses said to the Lord: "Oh, what a great sin these people have committed! They have made themselves gods of gold. But now, please forgive their sin—but if not, *then blot me out of the book you have written*" (Exodus 32:31-32, NIV).

This pleased the Lord, and He spared them. By offering himself as a sacrifice for a sinful nation, Moses was actually foreshadowing Jesus, who would give His life as a ransom for the world. And I can imagine God saying to him, "Moses, you remind Me of My Son."

Moses had come such a long way from the impetuous young Prince of Egypt, or the passive old man in the desert, watching the bush burn. He was now God's man, God's intercessor, and God's friend. He was beloved of the Lord.

But Moses' amazing conversation with the Lord wasn't over.

God told Moses that He would not destroy the people, but that He wouldn't go with them, either! Instead, He would send an angel to accompany them.

When Moses relayed this message to the nation, the people were devastated. They stripped off all the jewelry and ornaments and fancy trinkets they had packed out of Egypt and repented before the Lord.

And Moses, still in his role as intercessor for the people, went on negotiating with the Lord.

> Moses said to the Lord, "You have been telling me, 'Take these people up to the Promised Land.' But you haven't told me whom you will send with me. You call me by name and tell me I have found favor with you. Please, if this is really so, show me your intentions so I will understand you

more fully and do exactly what you want me to do. Besides, don't forget that this nation is your very own people."

And the LORD replied, "I will personally go with you, Moses. I will give you rest—everything will be fine for you."

Then Moses said, "If you don't go with us personally, don't let us move a step from this place. If you don't go with us, how will anyone ever know that your people and I have found favor with you? How else will they know we are special and distinct from all other people on the earth?"

And the LORD replied to Moses, "I will indeed do what you have asked, for you have found favor with me, and you are my friend." (Exodus 33:12-17, NLT)

The Lord was "drawing Moses out" as they spoke to each other. And He will do the same with us at different times in our lives.

We'll encounter a roadblock that stops us in our tracks. Bad news from the doctor…the job that didn't open…the deal that didn't close…the phone call that never came…the romantic relationship that never gelled…and sometimes you feel like you're losing hope.

Don't give up!

Press on. Press in. Keep praying, keep asking.

Remember Abraham, pleading with the Lord to turn back His impending judgment on the evil city of Sodom?

The LORD remained with Abraham for a while. Abraham approached him and said, "Will you destroy both innocent and guilty alike? Suppose you find fifty innocent people there within the city—will you still destroy it, and not spare it for their sakes? Surely you wouldn't do such a thing, destroying the innocent with the guilty. Why, you would be treating the innocent and the guilty exactly the same! Surely you wouldn't do that! Should not the Judge of all the earth do what is right?"

And the LORD replied, "If I find fifty innocent people
in Sodom, I will spare the entire city for their sake."
(Genesis 18:22-26, NLT)

Abraham kept the negotiating session going. If the Lord
had responded to the number of 50, would He respond to 45?
He would. And so it went, from 40 to 30 to 20…and finally to
10—as far as the patriarch dared to go.

It might almost seem irreverent the way Abraham "dickered"
with the Lord in this conversation. In reality, however, it reveals
the closeness of their friendship. It's also a reflection of the way
business was done in the Middle East. You always bargained for
a deal, never paying the original asking price.

Abraham was doing business with the Lord, and the most
significant point about this conversation was that *he already knew
he had the heart of the Lord in this prayer.* He could pray and
plead with God in confidence, knowing that He was just and merciful, a God who truly didn't want to bring calamity on people.[68]

Moses was doing business with the Lord, too—and he also
understood the heart of God with his requests.

1. he asks for divine direction.

"Now therefore, I pray, if I have found grace in Your sight,
show me now Your way." (Exodus 33:13)

This is really a prayer for every believer. In Moses' case,
he needed further revelation about God's intentions for the
future. *What next, Lord?*

God's reply in verse 14 is beautiful in its simplicity: "My
presence will go with you, and I will give you rest."

The Hebrew term for "presence" here is especially vivid.
God literally said, *"My face will go with you."* To give rest
doesn't mean that Moses and Israel would cease from activity,
but rather that they would enjoy God's protection and blessing.
A loose paraphrase might read, *"Don't sweat the small stuff.
I will take care of you."*

Just think how much time we waste in worry and fretting about things that never happen—how much needless energy we expend striving in our own strength to do what God has already promised to do for us.

It is said that worry is the interest paid on trouble before it's due! Worry does not empty tomorrow of it's sorrow…it empties today of its strength.

2. he asks for confirmation.

> Then he said to Him, "If Your Presence does not go with us, do not bring us up from here. For how then will it be known that Your people and I have found grace in Your sight, except You go with us?" (Exodus 33:15-16)

This may sound like Moses was lacking in faith, but it was really a good thing for him to express to the Lord. In essence, he was saying, "Lord, I don't want to make this journey without You. *I must have this assurance.*" Though the Lord had promised to send His angel before them, Moses wouldn't settle for that. He didn't want angels—whether one or a thousand—he wanted *God*.

I think this was pleasing to the Lord.

There was an occasion in the gospel of John where Jesus laid out what it really meant to follow Him. May of His so-called "disciples" bailed that day. As He watched these former followers walk away, Jesus turned to Peter and the others and said, "Will you also leave Me?"

> Simon Peter answered him, "Lord, to whom shall we go? You have the words of eternal life. We believe and know that you are the Holy One of God." (John 6:68-69, NIV)

"Lord, we don't know all that much, but this much we do know—we're staying with You!"

Do you want Jesus Christ to go with you in all you say and do? Sure, we might ask Him to accompany us when we're taking that long plane flight. We figure that if He's on board, we won't go

down! Or we may want Him to go with us to that job interview…
or into the operating room…or through that dangerous part of
town after dark.

But do we also want Him to go with us on our vacation…or
our night out with friends? Do we want Him to accompany us
to that party or movie? If we would be ashamed or embarrassed
for Him to see what we are seeing or doing, we shouldn't be
doing it in the first place.

God reassured His friend Moses with these words: "I will
also do this thing that you have spoken; for you have found
grace in My sight" (v. 17).

By this time Moses figures he's on a roll. Everything he's
asked for he has received. So he figures he may as well go f
or the gold.

3. he prays for the glory of GOD to be revealed to him.

And he said, "Please, show me Your glory." (v. 18)

Do you understand what Moses was asking for here? "Lord,
I want to *see* Your glory. *I want to see You!*"

Did Moses overstep his bounds here? Did he take too many
liberties with the Lord? Was God about to squash him like a
bug against the rocky walls of Sinai?

Not at all. Not only was this not a bad thing for Moses
to seek, it was a very good thing. Jesus Himself said, "If anyone
loves me, he will obey my teaching. My Father will love him, and
we will come to him and make our home with him" (John 14:23,
NIV). Again, in the book of Revelation, He declared: "Look! I have
been standing at the door, and I am constantly knocking. If anyone hears me calling him and opens the door, I will come in and
fellowship with him and he with me" (Revelation 3:20, TLB).

Moses was a man who came to understand the principle
objective of prayer. It's not just about "getting things" from the
Lord, it's about getting *the Lord Himself.*

In Chapter 5, we saw how the conniving, scheming Jacob finally met his match when the Lord Himself "wrestled with him until the breaking of day." Needless to say, Jacob lost that match, but in the process, an amazing thing happened to him. Jacob went from resisting to resting, from cunning to clinging. He had the Lord in the best wrestling hold he could think of, and he said to Him, "I will not let You go until You bless me!"

Here was a man who had come to understand prayer's true objective.

"Lord, whatever You want is fine by me—I just want You! I don't want to go even one step further in life without You right beside me."

Have you come to a point in your life where you are able to say to Jesus, "Your kingdom come, Your will be done, on earth as it is in heaven"? Or are you essentially praying, "Not Your will, but *mine* be done"?

We must never be afraid to place an unknown future into the hands of a known God. D. L. Moody counseled, "Spread out your petition before God, and then say, 'Thy will, not mine, be done.'" Later in life, Moody reflected, "The sweetest lesson I have learned in God's school is to *let the Lord choose for me.*"

God could not grant Moses all that he wanted, because seeing God in all His glory would have vaporized him. So the Lord worked out a special arrangement for His friend.

> Then He said, "I will make all My goodness pass before you, and I will proclaim the name of the LORD before you. I will be gracious to whom I will be gracious, and I will have compassion on whom I will have compassion." But He said, "You cannot see My face; for no man shall see Me, and live." And the LORD said, "Here is a place by Me, and you shall stand on the rock. So it shall be, while My glory passes by, that I will put you in the cleft of the rock, and will cover you with My hand while I pass by. Then I will take away My hand, and you shall see My back; but My face shall not be seen." (Exodus 33:19-23)

I can't begin to imagine what that experience must have been like. Moses must have felt like the apostle Paul, who after being caught up into heaven for a brief time, "heard inexpressible things, things that man is not permitted to tell."[69]

We think of Paul and Moses and Jacob, and we're awed by such a relationship with the living God. But do you realize that if you are a believer in Jesus Christ, you have a relationship with God that's *even closer*? Under the old covenant, only specially chosen men like Abraham and Moses had this kind of access into God's presence. Then, with the giving of the Law and the establishment of the Tabernacle—and later the Temple—God was to be approached only through the High Priest at particular times of the year by means of animal sacrifices.

Not just any person could stroll into the Holy of Holies and offer their prayer. If they tried, they would be struck down where they stood. Clearly, God did not *live in* His people at that time.

But all this changed with the death and resurrection of Jesus. He became our sacrifice, spilling His own blood on our behalf, and He is now interceding for us at the Father's right hand as our great High Priest.[70] When He died, the thick, heavy veil in the temple was ripped from top to bottom, because a new covenant had gone into effect…and the door into God's presence was thrown open wide.

We saw how, because of Moses, the people of Israel were spared. He interceded for them, and God turned away His wrath. In the same way, because of Jesus, we were spared. And now, because of His sacrifice, we have open access to God.

> And so, dear brothers, now we may walk right into the very Holy of Holies, where God is, because of the blood of Jesus. This is the fresh, new, life-giving way that Christ has opened up for us by tearing the curtain—his human body—to let us into the holy presence of God.

And since this great High Priest of ours rules over God's household, let us go right in to God himself, with true hearts fully trusting him to receive us because we have been sprinkled with Christ's blood to make us clean. (Hebrews 10:19-22, TLB)

Yes, Moses was God's friend.

But so are you.

Jesus said, "No longer do I call you servants, for a servant does not know what his master is doing; but I have called you friends, for all things that I heard from My Father I have made known to you" (John 15:15).

He is a Friend who walks with you through all of life. Let that thought strengthen you to resist the folly and sorrow of a compromised life. And let that thought strengthen you and give you courage as you walk step by step into an unknown future.

In the pages of this book, we've been considering "the greatest stories ever told." It's good to look back on lives that God has touched, transformed, refined, and used mightily for His kingdom. But it's even more important to realize that *your life* is a story—a story you're either beginning, right in the middle of, or about to finish. But no matter where you are in that journey, as you allow Jesus to transform you and His Holy Spirit to fill you, empower you, and use you, your life will also be a great story.

And the best is yet to come!

endnotes

1   Psalm 84:11

2   See 1 Timothy 2:14

3   Betsy Hart, *It Takes a Parent*

4   See Genesis 1:18; Proverbs 12:4, 18:22; 1 Corinthians 7:9

5   See Psalm 46:10

6   Acts 8:5-8, 26-40

7   James 4:2

8   Matthew 7:7, +

9   Genesis 25:23

10 Romans 12:18

11 Genesis 18

12 Joshua 5:13-15

13 Genesis 18

14 Deuteronomy 9:25-26

15 1 Kings 18:42-44

16 Psalm 39:12

17 Matthew 10:39

18 John 3:20, NIV

19 Luke 2:19, NLT

20 Proverbs 22:29

21 Proverbs 16:18

22 Genesis 39:6, NLT

23 James 4:7, NIV

24 2 Samuel 12:14, NLT

25 Dr. Lana Stanel, *Marital Infidelity*

26 Psalm 97:10, NIV

27 Psalm 51:4, NLT

28 Judges 16:6, NLT

29 1 Corinthians 10:13

30 James 3:16, NLT

31 1 Corinthians 3:3, NLT

32 Psalm 119:91, NIV

33 Exodus 8:19

34 Ephesians 4:27, NIV

35 2 Corinthians 2:11, NIV

36 Ecclesiastes 12:13, NIV

37 *Why The Ten Commandments Matter*,
    D. James Kennedy, Warner Books,
    New York, New York.

38   Exodus 3:14

39 1 Timothy 2:5

40 John 4:24

41 1 Timothy 6:8-10, NIV

42 2 Timothy 3:1, 4

43 Ephesians 5:12

44 1 Timothy 5:6

45 Luke 14:26

46 Read the full story in Luke 15:11-32.

47 Exodus 20:7

48 Exodus 6:7

49 Revelation 3:8, NLT

50 Romans 12:9, NLT

51 See John 19:30

52 Psalm 46:10

53 Mark 3:21

54 1 John 3:15, NLT

55 Ephesians 4:31-32, NIV

56 James 2:10, NIV

57 "The Thrill of Theft," by Jerry Adler,
   Newsweek, February 25, 2002.

58 Luke 19:8, NIV

59 The Day America Told the Truth,
   James Patterson and Peter Kim,
   Prentice Hall Trade; 1st edition (May 1991)

60 *Ibid.*

61 Hebrews 6:18

62 Exodus 32:30

63 John 19:11

64 Luke 12:48, NIV

65 Exodus 32:5

66 2 Samuel 12:10

67 John 4:48

68 See Jonah 4:2, and Lamentations 3:33

69 2 Corinthians 12:4, NIV

70 Romans 8:34; Hebrews 4:14-16; 9:24-28

about the author

greg Laurie is the pastor of Harvest
Christian Fellowship (one of
America's largest churches) in Riverside,
California. He is the author of over thirty
books, including the Gold Medallion Award
winner, *The Upside-Down Church*, as well
as *Every Day with Jesus; Are We Living
in the Last Days?; Marriage Connections;
Losers and Winners, Saints and Sinners;*
and *Dealing with Giants.* You can find his
study notes in the *New Believer's Bible*
and the *Seeker's Bible.* Host of the *Harvest:
Greg Laurie* television program and the
nationally syndicated radio program, *A
New Beginning*, Greg Laurie is also the
founder and featured speaker for Harvest
Crusades—contemporary, large-scale
evangelistic outreaches, which local
churches organize nationally and interna-
tionally. He and his wife Cathe live
in Southern California and have two
children and one grandchild.

Other AllenDavid books Published by Kerygma Publishing

The Great Compromise

For Every Season: Daily Devotions

Strengthening Your Marriage

Marriage Connections

Are We Living in the Last Days?

"I'm Going on a Diet Tomorrow"

Strengthening Your Faith

Deepening Your Faith

Living Out Your Faith

Dealing with Giants

Secrets to Spiritual Success

How to Know God

10 Things You Should Know About God and Life

For Every Season, vol. 2

Visit: www.kerygmapublishing.com
www.allendavidbooks.com
www.harvest.org